Bond
No.1 for exam success

English

Assessment Papers

9–10 years

Book 1

OXFORD
UNIVERSITY PRESS

OXFORD
UNIVERSITY PRESS

Great Clarendon Street, Oxford, OX2 6DP, United Kingdom

Oxford University Press is a department of the University of Oxford.
It furthers the University's objective of excellence in research, scholarship,
and education by publishing worldwide. Oxford is a registered trade mark of
Oxford University Press in the UK and in certain other countries

British Library Cataloguing in Publication Data
Data available

978-0-19-277646-4

10 9 8 7 6 5 4 3 2 1

Paper used in the production of this book is a natural, recyclable
product made from wood grown in sustainable forests.
The manufacturing process conforms to the environmental
regulations of the country of origin.

Printed in China

Acknowledgements

The publishers would like to thank the following for permissions to
use copyright material:

Page make-up: OKS Prepress, India
Illustrations: Nigel Kitching
Cover illustrations: Lo Cole

P6 'Give Yourself a Hug' copyright © Grace Nichols 1994 reproduced
with permission of Curtis Brown Group Ltd; p8 'A Week of Winter
Weather' by Wes Magee reproduced by permission of the author; p27
'The Night Mail' by W H Auden from *Collected Poems* reproduced by
permission of Faber and Faber Ltd; p33 'The Hyena and the Dead Ass'
retold by Rene Guillot, from *The Children of the Wind* selected and
translated by Gwen Marsh. Oxford University Press 1964, English
translation copyright © Oxford University Press; p48 extract from
The BFG by Roald Dahl published by Jonathan Cape Ltd & Penguin
Books Ltd reprinted by permission of David Higham Associates and
Farrar, Straus & Giroux Inc.; p53 extract from *The Hobbit* by J R R Tolkien
© The J R R Tolkien Estate Limited 1937, 1965. Reproduced by permission
of HarperCollins Publishers Ltd; p62 'The Sound Collector' by Roger
McGough from *Pillow Talk* copyright © Roger McGough 1990. Reproduced
by permission of Peters Fraser & Dunlop (www.petersfraserdunlop.com)
and United Agents on behalf of Roger McGough.

Although we have made every effort to trace and contact all
copyright holders before publication this has not been possible in all
cases. If notified, the publisher will rectify any errors or omissions at
the earliest opportunity.

Links to third party websites are provided by Oxford in good faith
and for information only. Oxford disclaims any responsibility for
the materials contained in any third party website referenced in
this work.

Before you get started

What is Bond?

This book is part of the Bond Assessment Papers series for English, which provides **thorough and continuous practice of key English skills** from ages five to thirteen. Bond's English resources are ideal preparation for Key Stage 1 and Key Stage 2 SATs, the 11+ and other selective school entrance exams.

What does this book cover and how can it be used to prepare for exams?

English 9-10 Book 1 and *Book 2* can be used both for general practice and as part of the run up to 11+ exams, Key Stage 2 SATs and other selective exams. The papers practise comprehension, spelling, grammar and vocabulary work. The coverage is also matched to the National Curriculum and the National Literacy Strategy. It is outside the scope of this book to practise extended and creative writing skills. *Bond Focus on Writing* provides full coverage of writing skills.

What does the book contain?

- **12 papers** – each one contains 100 questions.

- **Tutorial links throughout** – – this icon appears in the margin next to the questions. It indicates links to the relevant section in *How to do 11⁺ English*, our invaluable subject guide that offers explanations and practice for all core question types.

- **Scoring devices** – there are score boxes in the margins and a Progress Chart on page 64. The chart is a visual and motivating way for children to see how they are doing. It also turns the score into a percentage that can help decide what to do next.

- **Next Steps Planner** – advice on what to do after finishing the papers can be found on the inside back cover.

- **Answers** – located in an easily-removed central pull-out section.

How can you use this book?

One of the great strengths of Bond Assessment Papers is their flexibility. They can be used at home, in school and by tutors to:

- set **timed formal practice** tests – allow about 45 minutes per paper. Reduce the suggested time limit by five minutes to practise working at speed.

- provide **bite-sized chunks** for regular practice

- highlight **strengths and weaknesses** in the core skills

- identify **individual needs**

- set **homework**

- follow a **complete 11+ preparation strategy** alongside *The Parents' Guide to the 11+* (see below).

It is best to start at the beginning and work though the papers in order. If you are using the book as part of a careful run-in to the 11+, we suggest that you also have four other essential Bond resources close at hand:

How to do 11⁺ English: the subject guide that explains all the question types practised in this book. Use the cross-reference icons to find the relevant sections.

Focus on Comprehension: the practical handbook that clearly shows children how to read and understand the text, understand the questions and assess their own answers.

Focus on Writing: the essential resource that explains the key components of successful writing.

The Parents' Guide to the 11+: the step-by-step guide to the whole 11+ experience. It clearly explains the 11+ process, provides guidance on how to assess children, helps you to set complete action plans for practice and explains how you can use *English 9-10 Book 1* and *Book 2* as part of a strategic run-in to the exam.

See the inside front cover for more details of these books.

What does a score mean and how can it be improved?

It is unfortunately impossible to predict how a child will perform when it comes to the 11⁺ (or similar) exam if they achieve a certain score on any practice book or paper. Success on the day depends on a host of factors, including the scores of the other children sitting the test. However, we can give some guidance on what a score indicates and how to improve it.

If children colour in the Progress Chart on page 64, this will give an idea of present performance in percentage terms. The Next Steps Planner inside the back cover will help you to decide what to do next to help a child progress. It is always valuable to go over wrong answers with children. If they are having trouble with any particular question type, follow the tutorial links to *How to do 11⁺ English* for step-by-step explanations and further practice.

Don't forget the website…!

Visit www.bond11plus.co.uk for lots of advice, information and suggestions on everything to do with Bond, the 11+ and helping children to do their best.

Key words

Some special words are used in this book. You will find them in **bold** each time they appear in the Papers. These words are explained here.

abbreviation	a word or words which are shortened
abstract noun	a word referring to a concept or idea *love*
acronym	a word or letter string made up from the initial letters of other words
adjectival phrase	a group of words describing a noun
adjective	a word that describes somebody or something
adverb	a word that gives extra meaning to a verb
alphabetical order	words arranged in the order found in the alphabet
antonym	a word with a meaning opposite to another word *hot – cold*
clause	a section of a sentence with a verb
collective noun	a word referring to a group *swarm*
compound word	a word made up of two other words *football*
conjunction	a word used to link sentences, phrases or words *and, but*
connective	a word or words that join clauses or sentences
contraction	two words shortened into one with an apostrophe placed where the letter/s have been dropped *do not = don't*
definition	a meaning of a word
dialect	regional variation of vocabulary in the spoken language
diminutive	a word implying smallness *booklet*
future tense	form of a verb showing something that will or may happen
homophone	a word that has the same sound as another but a different meaning or spelling *right/write*
metaphor	an expression in which something is described in terms usually associated with another *the sky is a <u>sapphire</u> sea*
modal verb	a verb that changes the meaning of other verbs, for example can, will
noun	a word for somebody or something
onomatopoeic	a word that echoes a sound associated with its meaning *hiss*
parenthesis	this is a word or phrase that is separated off from the main sentence by brackets, commas or dashes usually because it contains additional information not essential to its understanding
past tense	form of a verb showing something that has already happened
personal pronoun	a pronoun used when writing about ourselves *I, you*
phrase	a group of words that act as a unit
plural	more than one *cats*
possessive pronoun	a pronoun showing to whom something belongs *mine, ours, his, hers, yours, theirs*
prefix	a group of letters added to the beginning of a word *un, dis*
preposition	a word that relates other words to each other – *he sat <u>behind</u> me, the book <u>on</u> the table*
present tense	form of a verb showing something happening now
pronoun	a word used to replace a noun
proper noun	the names of people, places etc. *Ben*
relative clause	a special type of clause that makes the meaning of a noun more specific, for example The prize *that I won* was a book
reported speech	what has been said, without using the exact words or speech marks
root word	a word to which prefixes or suffixes can be added to make another word <u>quick</u>ly
singular	one *cat*
suffix	a group of letters added to the end of a word *ly, ful*
synonym	a word with the same or very similar meaning to another word *quick – fast*
verb	a 'doing' or 'being' word

1

This is part of an old recipe to make rock cakes.

After you have spread the clean cooking cloth on the table, you must get together the ingredients. You will want:

6 ounces flour
2 ounces currants
1 egg   5
2 ounces butter
3 ounces castor sugar
1 teaspoon baking powder
$\frac{1}{2}$ teaspoon ground ginger
1 dessert spoonful milk   10

If you have any nice Beef Dripping you can use that instead of the butter, or you could use margarine, but butter is best.

Weigh the ingredients on the kitchen scales, and be careful to see that you have just the right quantity of everything.

Getting the oven ready   15

Now you had better light your oven gas, as you will want it hot by the time the cakes are ready to go in. (If you are cooking by a kitchen range, you will not have to do this, as your oven will be already getting hot, I expect.) Don't turn on the tap until you have got your matches in your hand, as we don't want the gas to escape. Open the door, turn on the tap, and light the rows of jets, gently, and close the door again.   20

Cleaning the currants

Then clean your currants. This is the best way. Put them into a basin with tepid water, and wash them. Pour the water away through a colander, so as not to pour away the currants and, with fresh water, give them a second wash. Pour this away, and rub the currants in a clean cloth. After that, put them into the oven on a plate   25
for a few minutes, to finish drying. You don't want the oven hot for this, as you do not want the currants cooked yet. So if you have been very quick about them, and you put the plate on a low shelf, which is cooler than the top of the oven, that will probably be just right.

If the oven has got hot before your currants are ready, you must turn the gas very   30
low while they are drying. They must be quite dry, without being cooked. The reason you have to be so particular is that your cakes will be more likely to be heavy if you do not put the fruit in quite dry.

Once the currants are dry take them out and pick them. By that I mean, take the stalks off. Some will have come off when you rubbed the currants in the cloth.   35

Mixing and beating

Put the flour into the bowl, with the baking powder, and mix well with a wooden spoon. Next, holding the butter between the thumb and first finger of your left hand, shred it – or cut it into thin slices – and let it drop into the flour. With the tips of your fingers rub the butter into the flour. Keep on working it about with your fingers   40
until there are no lumps at all, but the mixture feels like breadcrumbs. Now add the sugar, currants and ginger, and mix all well together.

Beat up your egg with an egg whisk or a fork, or some people use a knife, until it is frothy. Add this to the mixture and beat well. Put the milk into the cup in which you have beaten the egg – so as not to waste any of the egg – and then add that to the   45
basin. Keep on beating until all the ingredients are well mixed. The mixture should be quite stiff, and not at all liquid.

Underline the correct answers.

1 (Margarine, Butter, Beef dripping) is best to use when making rock cakes.

2 What might escape if the tap is turned on too soon? (water, gas, air)

3 (Sugar and flour, Sugar and ginger, Baking powder and sugar) are added to the fat and flour mixture with the currants.

3

Answer these questions.

4 The author describes in detail why it is so important for the currants to be dry. What do you think the word 'heavy' (line 33) means in this context?

_____

5–6 Copy two examples from the passage that show this recipe was written nearly 100 years ago.

_____

_____

7–10 Rewrite the 'Cleaning the currants' section as simply as possible in four steps.

_____

_____

_____

_____

7

3

Underline the correct **homophone** in each bracket.

11–12 The (scent, sent) of the flowers you (scent, sent) me is strong.

13–14 Tom (threw, through) the ball (threw, through) the window.

15–16 The (not, knot) joining these ropes is (not, knot) tied tightly.

17–18 Michelle cut her hand on the (pain, pane) of glass and she was in great (pain, pane).

19–20 I saw him (stair, stare) at the man on the (stairs, stares).

Circle the silent letter in each of these words.

21 cupboard

22 wreckage

23 budget

24 switch

25 thumbnail

26 column

Add the missing commas to these sentences.

27–29 Sam loved going for walks swimming in the duck pond chasing rabbits chewing a bone and sleeping in front of the fire.

30–31 The baby cries when it is tired hungry has a tummy ache or has a dirty nappy.

32–34 Jack wanted a new bike some colouring pens a computer game new trainers and a pet dog for his birthday!

Circle the **nouns**, including **proper nouns**.

35–41 gatepost fetched York Monday

bunch banana under frighten

fought violin team sunny

Choose an **adverb** to fill each gap. Each **adverb** may be used only once.

suddenly neatly heavily soundly

smartly greedily swiftly

42 Kim _____ wrote a letter.

43 The old tramp _____ ate his food.

44 All day the rain fell _____.

45 The child slept _____.

46 The boy ran _____ in the race.

47 The car braked _____.

48 The young woman always dressed _____.

Write the **plural** form of each of these **nouns**.

49 telephone _____   **50** thief _____

51 museum _____   **52** church _____

53 tragedy _____   **54** roof _____

Add the missing punctuation at the end of each sentence.

55 Watch out, James is coming_____

56 Many people had left their homes_____

57 It must be time to have dinner_____

58 Where has your Grandad gone_____

59 Why do I have to brush my teeth every day_____

60 The snow dropped silently, covering the ground_____

61 Quick, the film is about to start_____

Rewrite these sentences changing them from **plural** to **singular**.

62–64 The girls ran to catch their buses.

_____

65–66 They had collected money to give to the homeless children.

_____

67–69 The lambs bounced towards their mothers.

_____

Underline the **pronouns** in the following passage.

70–75 We are going to Hull to see the docks. We will see several ships and if we are
lucky they might let us look around them.

7

E 2

6

D 5

7

E 2

8

D 6

6

5

Underline one word in each group which is *not* a **synonym** for the rest.

76 hold   maintain   keep   destroy   retain

77 beautiful   nasty   lovely   pretty   handsome

78 happy   unwell   sick   ill   unhealthy

79 disagree   willing   differ   opposite   dissent

80 unhappy   sad   gloomy   upset   delighted

81 gigantic   enormous   big   tiny   large

6

Give Yourself a Hug

Give yourself a hug
when you feel unloved

Give yourself a hug
when people put on airs
to make you feel a bug   5

Give yourself a hug
when everyone seems to give you
a cold-shoulder shrug

Give yourself a hug –
a big big hug   10

And keep on singing
'Only one in a million like me
Only one in a million-billion-trillion-zillion
like me.'

by Grace Nichols

Answer these questions.

82 Which line in the poem repeats itself four times? _____

83–84 Write two reasons listed in the poem, why you should 'give yourself a hug'.

_____

_____

85 What is the meaning of 'a cold-shoulder shrug' on line 8 of the poem?

_____

86–87 What point is the poet making in the final verse? Use evidence from this verse to support your answer.

_____

_____

6

Write each of these words as an **adjective** by adding the **suffix** *ful*.

D 6
E 2

88 care   _____   **89** duty   _____

90 plenty   _____   **91** beauty   _____

92 wonder   _____

5

Copy each of these **phrases** making each **singular noun** plural.

Don't forget to add the missing apostrophe.

E 2
D 5

93–94 the three dog collars   _____

95–96 the two cinema screens   _____

97–98 the three boy books   _____

99–100 the two house chimneys   _____

8

Now go to the Progress Chart to record your score!   Total   100

A Week of Winter Weather

On Monday icy rain poured down
and flooded drains all over town.
Tuesday's gales bashed elm and ash;
dead branches came down with a crash.
On Wednesday bursts of hail and sleet,   *5*
no-one walked along the street.
Thursday stood out clear and calm
but the sun was paler than my arm.
Friday's frost that bit your ears
was cold enough to freeze your tears.   *10*
Saturday's sky was ghostly grey;
we smashed ice on the lake today.
Christmas Eve was Sunday ... and
snow fell and fell across the land.

by Wes Magee

Underline the correct answers.

1 On which day was there flooding?

(Monday, Wednesday, Friday)

2 On which day were we told there was no wind?

(Wednesday, Thursday, Saturday)

3 Which day of the week was Christmas Day?

(Sunday, Monday, Tuesday)

3

Answer these questions.

4–5 Pick out the two lines which describe the effect the weather has on the trees.

_____

_____

6–8 Write a word in the poem that rhymes with each of the following words.

calm ＿＿＿＿＿＿＿＿＿   and ＿＿＿＿＿＿＿＿＿   grey ＿＿＿＿＿＿＿＿＿

9–10 The first two lines of the poem describe rain on a winter's day.

Rewrite these two lines describing rain on a summer's day.

＿＿＿

＿＿＿

Find seven different **verbs** in the poem 'A Week of Winter Weather' by Wes Magee.

11–17 ＿＿＿＿＿＿＿＿＿   ＿＿＿＿＿＿＿＿＿   ＿＿＿＿＿＿＿＿＿

＿＿＿＿＿＿＿＿＿   ＿＿＿＿＿＿＿＿＿   ＿＿＿＿＿＿＿＿＿

＿＿＿＿＿＿＿＿＿

Underline one **clause** in each of these sentences.

18 The goats pushed their way out of their pen because they had spotted some apples.

19 The cars raced past us while we waited at the side of the motorway.

20 Matthew's present was quickly hidden under the sofa as he came in through the door.

21 Some children wanted to go swimming even though the water was freezing.

22 The hat fitted perfectly but it was the wrong colour.

23 It started to rain heavily as darkness fell over the sleepy village.

Underline the **root word** for each of these words.

24 unhappy	**25** jumped	**26** quickly
27 displacement	**28** uncertain	**29** affix
30 untie	**31** stronger	**32** mistrusted

Match a word with the same letter string but a different pronunciation, to each of these words.

height   foot   have   cough

drought   both   move   flower

33 bough ＿＿＿＿＿＿＿＿＿   **34** weight ＿＿＿＿＿＿＿＿＿

35 boot ＿＿＿＿＿＿＿＿＿   **36** cave ＿＿＿＿＿＿＿＿＿

37 moth ＿＿＿＿＿＿＿＿＿   **38** love ＿＿＿＿＿＿＿＿＿

39 slower ＿＿＿＿＿＿＿＿＿   **40** thought ＿＿＿＿＿＿＿＿＿

7

D 6

7

D 2

6

E 2

9

E 2

8

Copy these sentences and write a **possessive pronoun** in place of the words in bold.

D 6

41–42 Your hair looks longer than **my hair**. _____

43–44 Our house is smaller than **David's house**. _____

45–46 Their dog runs faster than **our dog**. _____

6

Write the masculine of each of the following words.

D 8

47 waitress _____   **48** aunt _____

49 queen _____   **50** niece _____

51 woman _____   **52** cow _____

53 vixen _____   **54** duchess _____

8

Add the missing *ie* or *ei* letters to complete each word correctly.

E 2

55 ch_____f   **56** f_____ld   **57** w_____ght

58 bel_____ve   **59** _____ght   **60** rec_____ve

61 v_____n   **62** th_____r

8

Copy the **proper nouns**, adding the missing capital letters.

D 6

63–69 duck   prince edward   wednesday

ship   london   football

everton football club   lucy smith   cargo

river severn   gate   parklands primary school

_____   _____

_____   _____

_____   _____

_____

7

Add a **verb** to these sentences. Each **verb** may be used only once.

D 6

Run   Watch   Pass   Stop   Find   Hurry

70 _____ me a drink!

71 _____ out, you're standing on my toe!

72 _____ yourself a chair and sit down.

73 _____, he is going to catch you!

74 _____, a car is coming!

75 _____ up, we will be late!

Write two **antonyms** for each of these words.

76–77 big _____ _____

78–79 rough _____ _____

80–81 sensible _____ _____

82–83 ugly _____ _____

84–89 Instructional texts give us information on how best to do something.

Clearly write out the most effective way to play a playground game or make a recipe of your choice.

You will be marked on the organisation and layout of your instructions as well as how clear and useful they are.

_____

_____

_____

_____

_____

_____

Change the degree of possibility in these sentences by adding a different modal verb to each one, for example The children *should* sit in their seats.

90 The children _____ sit in their seats.

91 The children _____ sit in their seats.

92 The children _____ sit in their seats

93 The children _____ sit in their seats.

94 The children _____ sit in their seats..

Write a word to match each clue.

95 A musical instrument with strings   c_____

96 Long pieces of pasta   s_____

97 An animal from Australia that jumps   k_____

98 A hot drink, often drunk at breakfast   c_____

99 A red fruit, often served in salad   t_____

100 What do you notice about the last letter of each of the words above (Q. 96–99)?

_____

6

Now go to the Progress Chart to record your score!   **Total**   100

Paper 3

I dared not stir out of my castle for days, lest some savage should capture me.
However, I gained a little courage and went with much dread to make sure that the
footprint was not my own. I measured my foot against it. Mine was not nearly so large.
A stranger, maybe a savage, must have been on shore, and fear again filled my heart.

    I determined now to make my house more secure than ever. I built another wall   5
around it, in which I fixed six guns, so that, if need be, I could fire off six in two minutes.
Then I planted young trees around. I feared my goats might be hurt or stolen from me,
so I fenced round several plots of ground, as much out of sight as possible, and put
some goats in each plot. All this while I lived with a terrible fear in my mind that I might
one day meet an enemy. I had lived on this lonely island for eighteen years.   10

    Once, when on the opposite side of the island, I was filled with horror; for on the
ground I saw the remains of a fire, and also a number of human bones. This told me
plainly that cannibals had been there.

From *Robinson Crusoe* by Daniel Defoe

Underline the correct answers.

1 How did Robinson Crusoe know the footprint was not his?
(it was a strange shape, it was larger than his, it was smaller than his)

2 How quickly could Robinson Crusoe fire his six guns?
(in 30 seconds, in one minute, in two minutes)

3 How long had Robinson Crusoe lived on the island?
(eighteen months, eight years, eighteen years)

◯ 3

Answer these questions.

4–5 Write the meaning of the words 'lest' (line 1) and 'plainly' (line 13) as they are used in this passage.

lest _____

plainly _____

6–7 How did Robinson Crusoe feel when he discovered cannibals were living on the island?

_____

Explain how you know this.

_____

8–10 Describe Robinson Crusoe's character in your own words.

Include lines or **phrases** from the text to support your answer.

_____

_____

_____

_____

_____

◯ 7

D 6

Underline the **nouns** in this passage.

11–21 My aunt, uncle and cousin came to stay with us last Wednesday. Next week we will catch a train to Birmingham. We are taking them to the theatre to see a pantomime called Aladdin. We will get back to our house very late.

◯ 11

Rewrite these sentences, adding the missing speech marks and other punctuation.

D 4
D 5

22–25 Come and hear the man play his banjo called Tim

_____

26–29 Where's my other slipper grumbled Grandpa

_____

8

D 11

Extend each of these words into a **compound word**.

30 tea_____   **31** sun_____

32 snow_____   **33** grand_____

34 pillow_____   **35** foot_____

36 tooth_____   **37** play_____

8

E 2

Write each of these words in its **plural** form.

38 brush   _____   **39** church   _____

40 child   _____   **41** valley   _____

42 thrush   _____   **43** baby   _____

6

D 12

Underline the **reported speech** sentences.

44–47 "Time to go Sam," called Mum.

Hank shouted to Ben to hurry up.

Kay moaned that Debbie was always late.

"Tuhil, are you coming?" shouted his teacher.

"Let's take the dog for a walk," pleaded the children.

The teacher told the children to leave by the fire exit.

"We had sausages for tea," said Maeve.

Mum told Gran that David's school report was good.

4

E 2

Rewrite these words adding the **suffix** _ing_ to each one.

48 drive   _____   **49** believe   _____

50 run   _____   **51** care   _____

52 close   _____   **53** refer   _____

54 transfer   _____   **55** canoe   _____

8

There is a lake near our town and it is very popular with both adults and children. The Sailing Club is at the south end of the lake and at the opposite end is a boathouse where visitors can hire various craft – sailing boats, rowing boats and canoes. Towards the middle of the lake on one side there is a part which is roped off. This is used for swimming. Sometimes a sailing boat capsizes, and as the water is not very deep this can provide much merriment for the onlookers! There are many reasons why a boat may capsize. Usually it is caused by a violent gust of wind, but it may be due to overloading, a faulty boat, or simply lack of skill in handling the craft.

Write *true* or *false* next to each statement.

56 The lake is only popular with children.   _____

57 The sailing club is at the north end of the lake.   _____

58 At the boathouse visitors can hire canoes.   _____

59 There is an area for swimming in the lake.   _____

60 The water in the lake is very deep.   _____

61 Overloading can cause boats to capsize.   _____

62 It is always the sailors' fault when a boat capsizes.   _____

Which creatures make these **onomatopoeic** noises?

63 Howl!   _____   64 Squawk!   _____

65 Snarl!   _____   66 Whinny!   _____

67 Coo   _____   68 Honk   _____

Add the missing commas to these sentences.

69 The wind swept over the barren landscape tossing leaves high into the air.

70 Although the speeding train came off its rails no one was hurt.

71 The lion crept up on its prey ready to pounce.

72–73 Reuben packed some snacks copying his sister to eat on the school trip.

74 Jess was delighted to see her mum though she wished she had come to collect her earlier.

Circle the words which have a soft *c*.

75–82 city   copy   cereal   face   magic   fleece

        clown   mice   lace   accident   cabbage

        vacuum   cat   jack   ace   carrot

With a line match the words with the same spelling patterns.

83 sound	match
84 high	hollow
85 fair	found
86 bridge	sigh
87 follow	fridge
88 hatch	chair

6

Rewrite each sentence as if you were writing about yourself.

D 6

Example: He enjoys running.   *I enjoy running.*

89 They fell over. _____

90 She feels hot. _____

91 He plays football. _____

92 They walk home slowly. _____

4

Add *cious* or *tious* to complete each word.

D 6

93 mali	_____	94 infec	_____
95 ficti	_____	96 deli	_____
97 suspi	_____	98 cau	_____
99 pre	_____	100 ambi	_____

8

A Servant for a Day by Kate Redman
23rd March

We arrived at Bourton House just after 10 o'clock. We were all dressed in Victorian costume. I was wearing a plain brown dress with black shoes and stockings. My hair was in a bun. I had a shawl to keep me warm.

    As soon as we arrived we were told off for being late. I thought it wasn't our fault but was too scared to say anything.

    Then we were given our instructions. We weren't allowed to talk, had to walk everywhere quietly and if we were spoken to, always had to say "Yes, ma'am" or "Yes, sir".

    We were shown into the dining room where we were taught to fold cotton napkins. It was very hard and Helen got told off for making a mess of hers.

    Then we went into the kitchens and were taught how to bake bread. We all took it in turns to help, it was great fun and the cook was really nice. She didn't mind if we talked and laughed.

    Suddenly we heard a bell in the corridor. The bell told us we were wanted in the bedrooms so we hurried up the stairs as quietly as possible. Dan fell over! There we were told how to make the bed and sweep the floor. When we swept the floor we had to put damp tea leaves down; as we swept them up it helped to pick up the dirt.

    At last it was time to go back to school. We were told we had been good servants and if we ever wanted a job we could have one at Bourton House!

    It was a great trip but I didn't like not being able to talk.

5

10

15

20

25

Underline the correct answers.

1 What period costume was Kate wearing?

(Viking, Victorian, Tudor)

2 Why did Kate wear a shawl?

(to look good, to hide her dress, to keep her warm)

3 Which room were they shown into first?

(the kitchen, the dining room, the bedroom)

4 Who got told off while folding a napkin?

(Helen, Kate, Dan)

4

Answer these questions.

5–6 Find two pieces of evidence from the text that suggest Victorian servants had to be quiet.

_____

_____

7–8 Which experience did Kate enjoy the most? Why?

_____

_____

9–11 Find three examples from the text that highlight the differences between Victorian times and now.

_____

_____

_____

7

Add the **prefix** *pro* or *bi* to each of these words.

E 2

| 12 _____lingual | 13 _____claim | 14 _____annual |
| 15 _____noun | 16 _____cycle | 17 _____longed |

6

Underline the correct form of the **verb** to complete each sentence.

D 6

18 The children watch/watches the match.

19 A cat play/plays with a mouse.

20 Winds sweep/sweeps across the land.

21 William run/runs to catch the bus.

22 The women win/wins the lottery.

23 Six children swim/swims for charity.

24 A leaf drop/drops from a tree.

⑦

Write one word for each **definition**.

25 Part of a plant that grows downwards and draws
food from the soil

_____

26 The time between dusk and dawn

_____

27 A grown-up person

_____

28 A member of the army

_____

29 A small white flower with a yellow centre

_____

30 A line of people, one behind another, waiting for their turn
to do something

_____

⑥

31–36 Write a short passage that includes at least two full stops, two question marks,
two exclamation marks and a pair of brackets.

D 5

_____

_____

_____

_____

_____

_____

⑥

B

> Squirrels are found in most countries. In Europe it is the red squirrel
> that is seen most, but in Britain the grey squirrel has been introduced
> from America. Flying squirrels do not really fly but glide from one tree
> to another. Ground squirrels may dig large numbers of burrows.

Underline the statements that are _true_ and circle the statements that are _false_.

37–43 There are only grey squirrels in Britain.

Flying squirrels glide.

Grey squirrels first came from America.

Squirrels are found in Europe and elsewhere.

There are not many squirrels now.

A ground squirrel's home is called a tunnel.

Flying squirrels live in America only.

Add a different **adjective** in each gap to complete the sentences.

44 The Browns had a _____ clock in the hall.

45 They made a _____ crown for the king.

46 The _____ lady presented the prizes.

47 They went up the _____ staircase.

48 The _____ book looked as though it had been read many times.

49 The _____ kitten romped around the house.

Write the word for the young of each of these animals.

50 dog _____   **51** pig _____

52 cat _____   **53** horse _____

54 cow _____   **55** goat _____

56 duck _____   **57** sheep _____

Rewrite these sentences without the double negatives.

58 I'm not never coming back.

_____

59 Mark hasn't brought no towel for swimming.

_____

60 The shopkeeper didn't have no fireworks.

_____

61 There wasn't no teacher to help with my spelling.

_____

62 Amy hasn't no coat to wear.

_____

63 There weren't no goats on the farm.

_____

Complete these word sums.

64 attend + ant = _____   **65** attend + ance = _____

66 assist + ant = _____   **67** assist + ance = _____

68 confide + ent = _____   **69** confide + ence = _____

70 correspond + ent = _____   **71** correspond + ence = _____

Add one of the **prefixes** to each word to make its **antonym**.

         un   in   im

72 _____expensive   **73** _____possible

74 _____kind   **75** _____mature

76 _____perfect   **77** _____done

Write whether these sentences are written in the **past**, **present** or **future** tense.

78 I am eating. _____

79 I will swim. _____

80 I am reading. _____

81 I ran home. _____

82 I will brush my teeth. _____

83 I have done my homework. _____

Underline the **conjunctions** in each sentence.

84 The river broke its bank and many houses were flooded.

85 Dan cut himself, however, he didn't need a plaster.

86 Rani felt unwell, nevertheless she still went to school.

87 Harry agreed to go to the playground though he really wanted to go straight home.

88 Kim was given a prize but Henry has never won one.

89 The children weren't tired although it was past their bedtime.

E 2
D 9

8

6

D 6

6

D 2

6

Write the **antonym** for each of these words.

90 near   _____   91 over   _____

92 top   _____   93 in   _____

94 day   _____   95 hot   _____

D 9
6

Circle the words which have a soft *g*.

E 2

96–100   gate   giraffe   vegetable   game

       gem   page   magic   goblin   wagon

5

Now go to the Progress Chart to record your score!   Total   100

Paper 5

Camouflage

B

Many animals are camouflaged by being of similar colour to the places where they live. The polar bear who lives in the snowy far north has white fur. The kangaroo, who lives in dry, dusty grassland, has sandy-coloured fur. The colour of the lion blends in with the colour of dry grass found in hot countries. The tapirs, who live in the jungles, have a colour pattern which seems of little use – the front of their   *5* bodies, their heads and their legs are black, while the rest is white. We can pick out tapirs easily at the zoo but in their homeland it is not so. They hunt at night when there are patches of moonlight and patches of shadow and this is how they are protected. Some animals, like the Arctic fox, who live in cold countries change the colour of their coats in winter so that the new white coat will tone in with the snow.   *10* Other animals have a dazzle pattern. A zebra's black and white stripes don't blend in with its surroundings, but zebras feed in the early morning and late evening when they cannot be seen so well. Their outline is broken up against the tall grasses and trees and they become almost invisible.

Underline the correct answers.

1 What colour is a polar bear's fur?

    (white, brown, sandy)

2 What environment does a kangaroo live in?

    (jungle, snowy far north, dry dusty grassland)

3–4 Which two animals are black and white?

    (polar bear, tapir, lion, Arctic fox, zebra)

4

Answer these questions.

5 Which animal lives in a hot country and has a coat the colour of dry grass?

_____

6 Two of the animals mentioned in the text are black and white. What else do they both have in common?

_____

7–8 What is interesting about the camouflage of the Arctic fox? Include a line from the text to support your answer.

_____

_____

_____

9 Write a **definition** for the word 'camouflage'.

_____

10 Why don't farm animals and pets need to be camouflaged?

_____

6

E 2

Change each of these **plurals** into its **singular** form.

11 churches   _____   **12** classes   _____

13 buses   _____   **14** bushes   _____

15 boxes   _____   **16** waltzes   _____

17 atlases   _____

18 Write a rule to be remembered when adding 'es' to make words plural.

_____

_____

8

D 6

Underline the **pronouns** in the sentences.

19–20 Mine is smaller than yours.

21–22 I am glad they have bought a dog.

23–24 You need to buy him a present.

25–26 Have you taken mine?

27–28 We have put ours over there.

10

Rewrite these book titles, adding the missing capital letters.

29–31 jason saves the day

_____

32–34 the history of the vikings

_____

35–38 football skills made fun

_____

D 6

10

Write a **synonym** for each of the words in bold.

D 9

39 The sailors were told to **abandon** the ship.   _____

40 The airman received an award for his **heroic** deed.   _____

41 I have **sufficient** money to buy it.   _____

42 She **enquired** how long she would have to wait.   _____

43 The **entire** school went on the outing.   _____

44 The children **dispersed** in all directions.   _____

45 The athlete **encountered** many difficulties.   _____

7

Add the missing apostrophes to each sentence.

D 5

46 Wheres your basket?

47 Isnt it over there?

48 Youll do it soon.

49 We shant do that!

50 I wont open the door.

51 We shouldve let her play with us.

52 Well have to go next time.

7

Put these towns in **alphabetical order**.

E 2

    Norwich   Northwich   Northampton

    Nottingham   Norwood   Northallerton

53 (1) _____   **54** (2) _____

55 (3) _____   **56** (4) _____

57 (5) _____   **58** (6) _____

6

Write five sentences, each with a relative clause beginning with the following words.

59 who _____

_____

60 that _____

_____

61 whom _____

_____

62 which _____

_____

63 whose _____

_____

5

Add the **suffix** to each of these words.

64 laugh + able _____ **65** response + ible _____

66 reason + able _____ **67** combust + ible _____

68 access + ible _____ **69** adore + able _____

70 consider + able _____ **71** sense + ible _____

8

Circle the **preposition** in each of these sentences.

72 The river flowed down the valley.

73 Karen hid behind the sofa.

74 Ethan and Meena struggled through the snow.

75 The zoo was behind the railway station.

76 Mum slept in the deckchair.

77 The cat jumped on the mouse.

78 The queen gracefully walked down the stairs.

79 The fish darted among the weeds.

8

REQUIRED IMMEDIATELY

A boy or girl to deliver newspapers

Hours – 6.30 a.m. to 8.00 a.m. Mondays to Saturdays

Wages £4 per day

It would be an advantage if the applicant had a bicycle

Write to:

Mr Jones

Newsagent

Pensby Rd

Moreton

Write *true* or *false* next to each of these statements.

80 The boy or girl must have a bicycle. _____

81 He/She would be needed six days a week. _____

82 Mr Jones wants a newsboy or girl quickly. _____

83 He/She would work nine hours a week. _____

84 Mr Jones doesn't mind if he employs a boy or a girl. _____

85 The pay would be £24 a week. _____

Write a word with the same letter string but a different pronunciation underlined in each of these words.

86 h<u>ear</u> _____ **87** e<u>igh</u>t _____ **88** thr<u>ough</u> _____

89 br<u>ave</u> _____ **90** <u>give</u> _____ **91** n<u>ow</u> _____

Add a powerful **verb** in the gaps to make each sentence interesting.

92 The children _____ over the bracken in their haste to get away.

93–94 Laila _____ at the top of her voice, making all the children

_____.

95 The cow _____ towards the milking parlour.

96 Sam _____ while watching the horror movie.

Write four words that have entered our language in the last hundred years.

97–100 _____ _____ _____ _____

Paper 6

The Night Mail

This is the Night Mail crossing the Border,
Bringing the cheque and the postal order,

Letters for the rich, letters for the poor,
The shop at the corner, the girl next door.

Pulling up Beattock, a steady climb: 5
The gradient's against her, but she's on time.
Past cotton-grass and moorland boulder,
Shovelling white steam over her shoulder,

Snorting noisily, she passes
Silent miles of wind-bent grasses.   10

Birds turn their heads as she approaches,
Stare from bushes at her blank-faced coaches.

Sheep-dogs cannot turn her course;
They slumber on with paws across.

In the farm she passes no one wakes,   15
But a jug in a bedroom gently shakes.

Dawn freshens. Her climb is done.
Down towards Glasgow she descends,
Towards the steam tugs yelping down a glade of cranes,
Towards the fields of apparatus, the furnaces   20
Set on the dark plain like gigantic chessmen.
All Scotland waits for her:
In dark glens, beside pale-green lochs,
Men long for news.

by W H Auden

Underline the correct answers.

1 Beattock is a (station, hill, shop).

2 Birds turn their heads (to see what is making the noise, because they like watching trains, because they have stiff necks).

3 'Blank-faced coaches' are (ones with no lights, ones painted black, ones with no curtains).

Answer these questions.

4–6 What three items are we told the train is carrying?

_____

7 Why do you think W H Auden describes the steam as 'over her shoulder'(line 8)?

_____

8 Give the meaning of the word 'descends' (line 18), as it is used in the poem.

_____

9 What image does the line 'Set on the dark plain like gigantic chessmen' (line 21) bring to mind?

_____

_____

10 Which line in the poem is evidence that there is a farm close to the railway track?

_____

_____

7

E 2

Underline the **root word** of each of these words.

11 pressure	**12** detective	**13** blacken
14 recovered	**15** signature	**16** freshly
17 swimming	**18** unhelpful	

8

D 6

Circle the word which is:

19 a **pronoun**	children	came	we	go
20 a **verb**	football	goal	play	boys
21 an **adjective**	dog	friend	him	sad
22 an **adverb**	speed	I	come	quickly
23 a **noun**	he	aunt	strong	enrage
24 a **pronoun**	there	though	through	it
25 a **verb**	teach	children	camera	dinner

7

Underline the correct **homophone**.

26 The (lessen, lesson) started at eleven o'clock.

27 The man gave a (groan, grown) as he lifted the weight.

28 Dad said we must get a new ironing (board, bored).

29 The (lone, loan) sailor had crossed the ocean.

30 The gardener put in (steaks, stakes) for the sweet peas to climb.

31 Kang had (two, to) help his teacher.

32 Alice had an (hour, our) to wait.

7

Which type of noun (**common**, **proper**, **abstract** or **collective**) is each of these words?

33 Anna _____   34 crowd _____

35 fence _____   36 love _____

37 flock _____   38 Brazil _____

39 sympathy _____

7

With a line match each expression with its meaning.

40 to be hard up   to be treated badly

41 to get into hot water   to take punishment without complaint

42 to have forty winks   to get into trouble

43 to go on all fours   to ask for trouble

44 to play with fire   to be short of money

45 to face the music   to crawl on hands and knees

46 to lead a dog's life   to have a short sleep

7

Complete each sentence by adding a **conjunction**.

47 She didn't see me _____ I waved at her.

48 I have learned to swim _____ I have been at this school.

49 I cannot reach my books _____ you have moved that parcel.

50 David likes his tea very hot _____ Brygid doesn't like tea at all.

51 I couldn't sing _____ I had a sore throat.

52 Kerry has cut her finger _____ she will have to wash it.

53 I am very keen on swimming _____ I like diving too.

7

Rewrite these words adding the **suffix** *ery* or *ary*. Make any spelling changes necessary.

E 2

54 burgle _____   **55** confection _____

56 jewel _____   **57** moment _____

58 slip _____   **59** diction _____

60 shrub _____   **61** bound _____

⬤ 8

D 6

Finish each sentence by adding a helper **verb** to match the **tense** in bold.

62 The car _____ speeding down the valley.   **past**

63 The birds _____ flying high in the sky.   **present**

64 A chicken _____ pecking in the dirt.   **present**

65 Two speed-boats _____ racing out to sea.   **past**

66 The sheep _____ flocking together on the moor.   **present**

67 A frog _____ jumping about in our pond.   **past**   ⬤ 6

D 5

Rewrite these sentences, adding the missing punctuation.

68–71 Can I have some of your drink asked Karen

_____

72–78 Are you up yet Jake's mum called It is time for school

_____

⬤ 11

D 8

Write the short form we often use for each of these words.

79 telephone _____   **80** bicycle _____

81 examination _____   **82** photograph _____

83 hippopotamus _____   **84** mathematics _____   ⬤ 6

1 **butter** Line 12 states that 'butter is best'.
2 **gas** Lines 18–19 state that you shouldn't 'turn on the tap until you have got your matches in your hand, as we don't want the gas to escape'.
3 **sugar and ginger** Lines 41–42 state 'Now add the sugar, currants and ginger, and mix all well together'.
4 *stodgy, lacking in air, hard*
5–6 *Now you had better light your oven gas' (line 16) and 'If you are cooking by a kitchen range…' (line 17). Also, the ingredients are measured in 'ounces' (lines 3–7).*
7–10 *Wash the currants in tepid water twice.*
Rub them with a cloth.
Put them in a warm oven to dry but not cook.
Once dry check all the currants have their stalks removed.
11–20 A homophone is a word that is pronounced the same as another, but has a different meaning or spelling.
11–12 **scent, sent** 'Scent' means a smell and if something has been 'sent', it has been dispatched.
13–14 **threw, through** 'Threw' is the past tense of throw, which means to propel something with force. 'Through' means passing from one side to another.
15–16 **knot, not** 'Knot' means a tie, and 'is not' is the negative of 'is'.
17–18 **pane, pain** A 'pane' is a single sheet of glass in a window frame, and 'pain' means hurt.
19–20 **stare, stairs** 'Stare' means to hold a gaze, while 'stairs' are steps.
21 cu**p**board
22 **w**reckage
23 bud**g**et
24 swi**t**ch
25 thum**b**nail
26 colum**n**
27–34 Commas are used to separate items in a list. There is a comma between each item except for the final two, which are separated by 'and' instead. Commas are also used to separate the main clause in a sentence from the additional added information.
27–29 Sam loved going for walks, swimming in the duck pond, chasing rabbits, chewing a bone and sleeping in front of the fire.
30–31 The baby cries when it is tired, hungry, has a tummy ache or has a dirty nappy.
32–34 Jack wanted a new bike, some colouring pens, a computer game, new trainers and a pet dog for his birthday!

35–41 A common noun is a person, place or thing. There are also proper nouns (the name of a person, place or thing) and collective nouns (the name of a group).
gatepost, York, Monday, bunch, banana, violin, team
42–48 Adverbs are words that give more information about the verb. The most appropriate adverbs need to be selected here, and there is only one correct adverb for each phrase.
42 Kim **neatly** wrote a letter.
43 The old tramp **greedily** ate his food.
44 All day the rain fell **heavily**.
45 The child slept **soundly**.
46 The boy ran **swiftly** in the race.
47 The car braked **suddenly**.
48 The young woman always dressed **smartly**.
49 **telephones** This word just needs an 's' added to make it plural
50 **thieves** The spelling rules is to change the 'f' to 'v' and then add 'es'.
51 **museums** This word just needs an 's' added to make it plural.
52 **churches** The spelling rule for words ending in 's', 'ss', 'ch', 'sh', 'x', 'z', or 'zz' is to add an 'es'
53 **tragedies** The spelling rule is to change the 'y' to 'i' and then add 'es'
54 **roofs** When words end in 'f', the 'f' is usually changed to 'v' and 'es' is added. However, there are exception to this rule and 'roofs' is one of them.
55 **Watch out, James is coming!** Use an exclamation mark to show something surprising or forceful.
56 **Many people had left their homes.** This is a statement so a full stop is needed to end it.
57 **It must be time to have dinner. / It must be time to have dinner!** This could be a statement or an exclamation, therefore either a full stop or an exclamation mark can be used here.
58 **Where has your Grandad gone?** This is a question so a question mark should be used here.
59 **Why do I have to brush my teeth every day?** This is a question so a question mark should be used here.
60 **The snow dropped silently, covering the ground.** This is a statement so a full stop is needed to end it.
61 **Quick, the film is about to start!** This is an exclamatory sentence, therefore an exclamation mark should be used.
62–64 **The girl ran to catch her bus.** 'Girl' is the singular form of 'girls'. To make the plural,

's' is added. 'Bus' is the singular form of 'buses'. To make the plural of a word ending in 's', 'es' is added. 'Their' is changed to the singular form of 'her'.

65–66 He/she had collected money to give to the homeless child. He/she is the singular form of they. Child is the singular form of children.

67–69 The lamb bounced towards its mother. Lamb is the singular form of lambs. To make the plural, 's' is added. Its is the singular form of their. Mother is the singular form of mothers. To make the plural, 's' is added.

70–75 Pronouns are words which replace nouns in a sentence to avoid repetition.
We are going to Hull to see the docks. **We** will see several ships and if **we** are lucky **they** might let **us** look around **them**.

76–81 Synonyms are words which have similar meanings as other words.

76 destroy hold, maintain, keep and retain are synonyms and mean to keep possession of something.

77 nasty beautiful, lovely, pretty and handsome are synonyms and mean attractive.

78 happy unwell, sick, ill and unhealthy are synonyms and are the opposite of healthy.

79 willing disagree, differ, oppose and dissent are synonyms and mean to argue against something.

80 delighted unhappy, sad, gloomy and upset are synonyms and mean miserable.

81 tiny gigantic, enormous, big and large are synonyms and mean huge.

82 Give yourself a hug This is repeated on lines 1, 3, 6 and 9.

83–84 Any two of: *When you feel unloved; when people put on airs; when people give a cold shoulder shrug.*

85 *When people ignore you.*

86–87 *The final verse emphasises how special each and every one of us is. 'Only one in a million-billion-trillion-zillion like me.'*

88–91 An adjective is a word that describes a noun. When adding the suffix 'ful', words ending 'y' have the 'y' changed to an 'i' before 'ful' is added (for example, beauty becomes beautiful).

88 careful
89 dutiful
90 plentiful
91 beautiful
92 wonderful

93–94 the three dogs' collars. The plural of 'dog' is 'dogs'. To show plural possession, an apostrophe is placed after the 's'.

95–96 the two cinemas' screens. The plural of 'cinema' is 'cinemas'. To show plural possession, an apostrophe is placed after the 's'.

97–98 the three boys' books. The plural of 'boy' is 'boys'. To show plural possession, an apostrophe is placed after the 's'.

99–100 the two houses' chimneys. The plural of 'house' is 'houses'. To show plural possession, an apostrophe is placed after the 's'.

Paper 2 (pages 8–12)

1 Monday Lines 1–2 state that 'On Monday icy rain poured down and flooded drains all over town'.

2 Thursday Line 7 states that 'Thursday stood out clear and calm'.

3 Monday Line 13 states that 'Christmas Eve was Sunday…'

4–5 *'Tuesday's gales bashed elm and ash; dead branches came down with a crash'.*

6–8 arm, land, today

9–10 The two lines need to rhyme and have a similar structure to the original poem, e.g. *On Monday the sun was out all day, so all the children went out to play.*

11–17 A verb is an action word. Any seven can be picked from the following verbs: *poured, flooded, bashed, came, walked, stood, was, bit, freeze, smashed, fell.*

18–23 A clause is a section of a sentence with a verb. There are two possible options in each of the below. In subordinate clauses the conjunction (e.g. because, while, as, although) is considered part of the clause, so can be underlined too. The conjunction is not considered part of the clause if it has joined two main clauses (e.g. and, but), so does not have to be underlined.

18 <u>The goats pushed their way out of their pen</u> because <u>they had spotted some apples.</u>

19 <u>The cars raced past us</u> while we waited at the side of the motorway.

20 <u>Matthew's present was quickly hidden under the sofa</u> as he came in through the door.

21 <u>Some children wanted to go swimming</u> even though the water was freezing.

22 <u>The hat fitted perfectly</u> but <u>it was the wrong colour.</u>

23 <u>It started to rain heavily</u> as darkness fell over the sleepy village.

24–32 A root word is a word to which prefixes or suffixes can be added to make another word. For example, *quick* is the root word of *quicker* and *quickly*.

24 un**happy**
25 **jump**ed
26 **quick**ly
27 dis**place**ment

A2

28 un**certain**

29 af**fix**

30 un**tie**

31 **strong**er

32 mis**trust**ed

33–40 A letter string is a group of letters that appear in many words, for example, 'thr' or 'ight'.

33 **cough**

34 **height**

35 **foot**

36 **have**

37 **both**

38 **move**

39 **flower**

40 **drought**

41–46 A possessive pronoun is a pronoun showing to whom something belongs. For example, words such as mine, ours, his, hers, yours and theirs are possessive pronouns.

41–42 **Yours** looks longer than **mine.**

43–44 **Ours** is smaller than **his.**

45–46 **Theirs** runs faster than **ours.**

47 **waiter**

48 **uncle**

49 **king**

50 **nephew**

51 **man**

52 **bull**

53 **fox**

54 **duke**

55–62 The spelling rule for these words are to place an 'i' before an 'e' unless after 'c' although there are some words (seize, weird, eight, neither, leisure, either for example) that are the exception to the rule.

55 **chief**

56 **field**

57 **weight** This is an exception to the spelling rule

58 **believe**

59 **eight** This is an exception to the spelling rule.

60 **receive**

61 **vein** This is an exception to the spelling rule.

62 **their** This is an exception to the spelling rule.

63–69 A proper noun is the name of a person, place or thing. Proper nouns always begin with a capital letter. If a proper noun has more than one word, then each word needs a capital letter.
Prince Edward, Wednesday, London, Everton Football Club, Lucy Smith, River Severn, Parklands Primary School

70 **Pass** me a drink!

71 **Watch** out, you're standing on my toe!

72 **Find** yourself a chair and sit down.

73 **Run,** he is going to catch you!

74 **Stop,** a car is coming!

75 **Hurry** up, we will be late!

76–83 An antonym is a word that has an opposite meaning to another word. For example, the word 'wet' is an antonym for the word 'dry'. There is often more than one word that could be an antonym. For example, 'wet' is also an antonym for the word 'arid'. There are therefore many possible answers.

76–77 Possible answers include: *small, tiny, miniscule, minute*

78–79 Possible answers include: *smooth, slippery, polished, shiny, delicate*

80–81 Possible answers include: *silly, foolish, immature, reckless*

82–83 Possible answers include: *pretty, beautiful, attractive, picturesque*

84–89 Marks are given for organisation and layout of information, as well as how clear and useful the instructions are. A possible answer could read:
Sit on the floor (or chairs) in a circle. Choose one child to walk around the outside of the circle, tapping each child on the head gently saying "Duck" each time. The child needs to tap one child's head saying "Goose!". The child whose head has been tapped needs to run in a clockwise direction around the circle, chasing the 'tapper'. If the runner is caught, the child chasing can return to their seat. If not, the child chasing becomes the new 'tapper'.

90–94 A modal verb is a word that expresses necessity or possibility. Possible words awarded marks here are: *must, shall, will, should, would, could, may* and *might*.

95 **cello**

96 **spaghetti**

97 **kangaroo**

98 **coffee**

99 **tomato**

100 *The last letter of each word is a vowel.*

Paper 3 (pages 2–16)

1 **It was larger than his** Line 3 states that 'Mine was not nearly so large'.

2 **in two minutes** Line 6 states that 'I could fire off six in two minutes'.

3 **eighteen years** Line 10 states that Robinson Crusoe 'had lived on this lonely island for eighteen years'.

4–5 *lest – in case; plainly – clearly*

6–7 *Robinson Crusoe was horrified/scared when he discovered cannibals were living on the island.*
We know this because he says that when he saw the human bones he was 'filled with horror' (lines 11–12).

8–10 Acceptable answers could include any of the following points: *Robinson Crusoe is resourceful because he has been able to survive on an island by himself 'for eighteen years'; he is terrified of being attacked ('All this while I lived with a terrible fear'); when faced with a challenge ('I feared my goats might be hurt or stolen') he comes up with a solution, building several hidden enclosures for the goats. He is brave and prepared to fight if he has to ('if need be, I could fire off six [guns] in two minutes').*

11–21 My **aunt**, **uncle** and **cousin** came to stay with us last **Wednesday**. Next **week** we will catch a **train** to **Birmingham**. We are taking them to the **theatre** to see a **pantomime** called **Aladdin**. We will get back to our **house** very late.

22–25 "Come and hear the man play his banjo," called Tim.

26–29 "Where's my other slipper?" grumbled Grandpa.

30–37 A compound word is a word formed from two other words. There are several options for each answer.

30 Possible answers include: *teaspoon, teacup, teatime, teapot, teabag*

31 Possible answers include: *sunshine, sunglasses, sunbathe, sunrise, sunset*

32 Possible answers include: *snowball, snowflake, snowstorm, snowboard, snowdrift, snowdrop*

33 Possible answers include: *grandfather, grandmother, grandchild, grandstand*

34 Possible answers include: *pillowcase*

35 Possible answers include: *football, footfall, footpath, foothold, footprint*

36 Possible answers include: *toothache, toothbrush, toothpaste*

37 Possible answers include: *playtime, playground, playmat, playgroup*

38 **brushes** The spelling rule is to add an 'es' to words ending in 'sh'.

39 **churches** The spelling rule is to add an 'es' to words ending in 'ch'.

40 **children** This an exception to the spelling rule of adding an 's' after a consonant.

41 **valleys** The spelling rule is to add 's' to the end.

42 **thrushes** The spelling rule is to add an 'es' to words ending in 'sh'.

43 **babies** The spelling rule is to change the 'y' to 'ies' for a word that ends in a consonant + 'y'.

44–47 Reported speech (indirect speech) refers to something being said without quoting the actual words. Phrases such as 'said that' and 'shouted to' are used, and the inverted commas (speech marks) are removed to show that it is not direct speech. In addition, the tense of the verb may sometimes change, for example from present to past.

Hank shouted to Ben to hurry up.
Kay moaned that Debbie was always late.
The teacher told the children to leave by the fire exit.
Mum told Gran that David's school report was good.

48–56 When a word has a short vowel sound (as in cat, met, fit, hop or shut), the consonant at the end of the word is doubled when adding a suffix. When a word has a long vowel sound (as in gave, part, feel, thrive, grove, shoot, cube, etc), remove the 'e' and add the suffix.

48 **driving** Drive has a long vowel sound, so remove the 'e' before adding 'ing'.

49 **believing** Believe ends in a long vowel sound, so remove the 'e' before adding 'ing'.

50 **running** Run has a short vowel sound, so double the last letter before adding 'ing'.

51 **caring** Care has a long vowel sound, so remove the 'e' before adding 'ing'.

52 **closing** Close has a long vowel sound, so remove the 'e' before adding 'ing'.

53 **referring** Refer is an exception to this rule and the 'r' is doubled.

54 **transferring** Transfer is an exception to this rule and the 'r' is doubled.

55 **canoeing** Canoe is an exception to this rule. It ends with 2 vowels in a long vowel sound, so 'ing' just needs to be added.

56 **false** The text states that the lake is popular 'with both adults and children'.

57 **false** The text states that the sailing club is at the 'south end of the lake'.

58 **true** The text states that visitors can hire 'sailing boats, rowing boats, and canoes.'

59 **true** The text states that there is a 'part which is roped off... for swimming'.

60 **false** The text states that the water 'is not very deep'.

61 **true** The text states that a boat could 'capsize... due to overloading'.

62 **false** The text states that when a boat capsizes it could be due to 'overloading' or a 'faulty boat' too.

63–68 A word that is onomatopoeic sounds like the word itself. Examples might include sizzle, pop, bang, hiss. There could be several different animals for each answer, but any sensible suggestions will be rewarded here. Possible answers include:

63 *dog, wolf*

64 *parrot, chicken*

65 *lion, dog*

66 *horse, pony, donkey*

67 *dove, pigeon*

68 *goose*

69–74 In these sentences, commas are needed to separate clauses, or surround additional information,

69 *The wind swept over the barren landscape, tossing leaves high into the air.* (A comma separates the main clause from the subordinate clause)

70 *Although the speeding train came off its rails, no one was hurt.* (A comma separates the subordinate clause from the main clause)

71 *The lion crept up on its prey, ready to pounce.* (A comma separates the main clause from the subordinate clause)

72–73 *Reuben packed some snacks, copying his sister, to eat on the school trip.* (Commas surround the additional information)

74 *Jess was delighted to see her mum, though she wished she had come to collect her earlier.* (A comma separates two main clauses)

75–82 A 'soft c' sounds like the letter 's' and is usually followed by the letters e, i or y. A hard 'c' sounds like the letter 'k' and is usually followed by the letters a, o or u.
city, cereal, face, fleece, mice, lace, accident, ace

83 **found**

84 **sigh**

85 **chair**

86 **fridge**

87 **hollow**

88 **match**

89 **I fell over.** To change to first person, change 'they' to 'I'. The rest remains the same.

90 **I feel hot.** To change to first person, change 'she' to 'I'. Then 'feels' becomes 'feel' (the correct verb following 'I').

91 **I play football.** To change to first person, change 'he' to 'I'. Then 'plays' becomes 'play'.

92 **I walk home slowly.** To change to first person, change 'they' to 'I'. Then 'walk' stays the same.

93–100 If the root word ends in 'ce' remove the 'e' and add 'ious'. For example, space becomes spacious. If the root word ends in 'tion', remove the 'tion' and replace with 'tious'. For example, nutrition becomes nutritious. However, in spelling there are exceptions to the rules: in this case words like anxious, suspicious and fictitious.

93 **cious** mali<u>cious</u> (malice)

94 **tious** infec<u>tious</u> (infection)

95 **tious** ficti<u>tious</u> (fiction)

96 **cious** deli<u>cious</u>

97 **cious** suspi<u>cious</u> (suspicion)

98 **tious** cau<u>tious</u> (caution)

99 **cious** precious (price)

100 **tious** ambi<u>tious</u> (ambition)

Paper 4 (pages 17–22)

1 **Victorian** Lines 3–4 state that 'We were all dressed in Victorian costume'.

2 **to keep her warm** Lines 5–6 state that 'I had a shawl to keep me warm'.

3 **the dining room** Line 12 states that 'we were shown into the dining room'.

4 **Helen** Lines 13–14 state that 'Helen got told off for making a mess of hers'.

5–6 *'We weren't allowed to talk' and 'had to walk everywhere quietly'.* (lines 9–10)

7–8 *Kate enjoyed learning how to bake bread because the cook was nice and allowed them to talk and laugh (lines 16–17).*

9–11 Answers could include: *servants, folding napkins, bell in corridor, sweeping the floor with tea leaves.*

12–17 The prefix 'bi-' generally means 'two' or 'double', whilst the prefix 'pro-' primarily means 'forward' but can also mean 'for'.

12 **bi** bilingual

13 **pro** proclaim

14 **bi** biannual

15 **pro** pronoun

16 **bi** bicycle

17 **pro** prolonged

18 The children **watch** the match.

19 A cat **plays** with a mouse.

20 Winds **sweep** across the land.

21 William **runs** to catch the bus.

22 The women **win** the lottery.

23 Six children **swim** for charity.

24 A leaf **drops** from a tree.

25 **root**

26 **night**

27 **adult**

28 **soldier**

29 **daisy**

30 **queue**

31–36 Full stops follow a statement or command. Question marks follow a question. Exclamation marks follow a sentence that is saying something surprising or forceful. Brackets surround any additional information. A possible answer could be:
Alice was starving! She had been waiting for three hours for her mum to get home from work (she was usually late!). Why did she always end up waiting for other people?
"Hi Mum!" she yelled, as her mother came through the door. "What are we having for dinner tonight?"

37 **False:** as the text states that 'in Britain the grey squirrel has been introduced from America' but does not imply that there are therefore no red squirrels there.

38 **True:** The text states that 'flying squirrels do not really fly but glide'.

39 **True:** the text states that 'the grey squirrel has been introduced from America'.

40 **True:** the text states that squirrels are found in 'most countries' and specifically, America, which is not in Europe.

41 **False:** they are found in 'most countries'.

42 **False:** the text states that their home is called a 'burrow'.

43 **False:** the text states that it is grey squirrels which come from America, not the flying squirrels.

44 *brown, tall, wooden*

45 *gold, attractive, precious*

46 *smart, impressive*

47 *rickety, steep*

48 *old, damaged*

49 *fluffy, cute*

50 **puppy**

51 **piglet**

52 **kitten**

53 **foal**

54 **calf**

55 **kid**

56 **duckling**

57 **lamb**

58–63 Double negatives are two negative words used in the same sentence. Using two negatives turns the sentence into a positive one (which is confusing). There may be more than one answer for some of the questions.

58 **I'm never coming back/I'm not ever coming back.**

59 **Mark hasn't brought a towel for swimming.**

60 **The shopkeeper didn't have any fireworks.**

61 **There wasn't a teacher to help with my spelling/There was no teacher to help with my spelling.**

62 **Amy hasn't a coat to wear/Amy has no coat to wear.**

63 **There weren't any goats on the farm/There were no goats on the farm.**

64 **attendant**

65 **attendance**

66 **assistant**

67 **assistance**

68 **confident** The spelling rule is to remove the 'e' from 'confide' before adding 'ent'.

69 **confidence** The spelling rule is to remove the 'e' from 'confide' before adding 'ence'.

70 **correspondent**

71 **correspondence**

72–77 A prefix is a group of letters that can be added to the beginning of a root word to make a new, sensible word. In this case, add a prefix to make the word its antonym. There is only one possible answer for each.

72 **in** inexpensive

73 **im** impossible

74 **un** unkind

75 **im** immature

76 **im** imperfect

77 **un** undone

78 **present** The words 'I am' show that it is happening now.

79 **future** The words 'I will' show that it is happening in the future.

80 **present** The words 'I am' show that it is happening now.

81 **past** The word 'ran' is the past tense of 'to run'.

82 **future** The words 'I will' show that it is happening in the future.

83 **past** The words 'have done' are the past tense of 'to do'.

84–89 A conjunction is a joining word such as 'and' or 'but' that joins two clauses together.

84 The river broke its bank **and** many houses were flooded.

85 Dan cut himself, **however**, he didn't need a plaster.

86 Rani felt unwell, **nevertheless** she still went to school.

87 Harry agreed to go to the playground **though** he really wanted to go straight home.

88 Kim was given a prize **but** Henry has never won one.

89 The children weren't tired **although** it was past their bedtime.

90–95 Possible answers:

90 *far, distant*

91 *under, below*

92 *bottom*

93 *out*

94 *night*

95 *cold, freezing*

96–100 A 'soft g' sounds like the letter 'j' and is usually followed by the letters e, i or y. A hard 'g' is pronounced like the 'g' in the word 'gate' and is usually followed by the letters a, o, or u. **giraffe, vegetable, gem, page, magic**

Paper 5 (pages 22–26)

1 **white** Line 2 states that 'the polar bear who lives in the snowy far north has white fur'.

2 **dry dusty grassland** Lines 2–3 state that 'the kangaroo, who lives in dry, dusty grassland…'

3–4 **tapir, zebra** Line 6 states that tapirs' 'heads and their legs are black, whilst the rest is white', whilst line 11 states that 'a zebra's black and white stripes don't blend..'.

5 *a lion (lines 3–4)*

6 *Both animals feed either when the light is low (dusk or dawn) or during the night.*

7–8 A possible answer could be:
The Arctic fox is interesting because it changes its coat to camouflage itself with the seasons. We know this because the text states: 'Some animals, like the Arctic fox, who live in cold countries change the colour of their coats in winter so that the new white coat will tone in with the snow.'

9 *a disguise, a way to hide*

10 *Farm animals and pets don't need to be camouflaged because they don't need to hide from predators.*

11–17 In all of these instances, the plural is created by adding 'es', so when changing from plural to singular, 'es' is removed.

11 **Church**

12 **Class**

13 **Bus**

14 **Bush**

15 **Box**

16 **Waltz**

17 **Atlas**

18 *When making words plural that end in ch, sh, s, ss, x, z or zz add 'es' (but remember there are always exceptions to the rule).*

19–20 **Mine** is smaller than **yours**.

21–22 I am glad **they** have bought a dog.

23–24 **You** need to buy **him** a present.

25–26 Have **you** taken **mine**?

27–28 **We** have put **ours** over there.

29–38 In book titles, the beginning of the title and all words besides prepositions and conjunctions should be capitalised.

29–31 **J**ason **S**aves the **D**ay

32–34 **T**he **H**istory of the **V**ikings

35–38 **F**ootball **S**kills **M**ade **F**un

39–45 A synonym is a word that has a similar meaning. Possible examples:

39 *leave*

40 *brave*

41 *enough*

42 *asked*

43 *whole*

44 *scattered*

45 *met, faced*

46 **Where's your basket?** The full sentence would read 'Where is your basket?' so an apostrophe is added in place of the 'i' in 'is'.

47 **Isn't it over there?** 'Isn't' is short for 'is not'. The apostrophe is added in the place of the 'o'.

48 **You'll do it soon.** 'You'll' is short for 'You will'. The apostrophe is added in to replace the 'wi'.

49 **We shan't do that.** 'Shan't' is short for 'shall not'. The apostrophe is added to replace the 'o'. The 'll' is lost.

50 I **won't** open the door. 'Won't' is a short version of 'will not'. The apostrophe is added in to replace the 'o'.

51 **We should've let her play with us.** 'Should've' is short for 'should have'. The apostrophe is added to replace the 'ha'.

52 **We'll have to go next time.** 'We'll' is short for 'we will'. The apostrophe is added to replace the 'wi'.

53–58 **Northallerton, Northampton, Northwich, Norwich, Norwood, Nottingham**

59–63 A relative clause is a clause that starts with a relative pronoun. Examples are: who, that, which, whose, where and when. They are most often used to define or identify the noun that precedes them. Here are some possible answers:

59 *The woman, who won the Marathon today, came second last year.*

60 *The bicycle that I rode belonged to Liam.*

61 *Ellie, whom I had never met before, looked just like my cousin.*

62 *The cat, which was hiding under the bed, was called Clarence.*

63 *The boy, whose party it was, cried.*

64 **laughable**

65 **responsible** The spelling rule when the root words ends in 'e' (response) is to drop the 'e' before adding 'able' or 'ible'.

66 **reasonable**

67 **combustible**

68 **accessible**

69 **adorable** The spelling rule when the root words ends in 'e' (adore) is to drop the 'e' before adding 'able' or 'ible'.

70 **considerable**

71 **sensible** The spelling rule when the root words ends in 'e' (sense) is to drop the 'e' before adding 'able' or 'ible'.

72–79 A preposition is a word that is used to give more information about a noun. It is used to describe the position, time or cause. In this case, the prepositions are used to describe the position.

72 The river flowed **down** the valley.

73 Karen hid **behind** the sofa.

74 Ethan and Meena struggled **through** the snow.

75 The zoo was **behind** the railway station.

76 Mum slept **in** the deckchair.

77 The cat jumped **on** the mouse.
78 The queen gracefully walked **down** the stairs.
79 The fish darted **among** the weeds.
80 **false** The text states that 'it would be an advantage if the applicant had a bicycle'.
81 **true** The text states 'Monday to Saturdays' which is six days.
82 **true** The word 'immediately' shows Mr Jones wants a newsboy or girl quickly.
83 **true** The hours are an hour and a half a day for six days which equates to nine hours a week.
84 **true** The text states 'a boy or girl…'
85 **true** The pay is £4 a day which equates to £24 a week.
86–91 There are several possible answers here for words with the same letter strings but different pronunciation. Below are a few possible answers.
86 *bear*
87 *height, bright*
88 *enough, bough, tough, though*
89 *have*
90 *dive, hive, five*
91 *tow, mow, low*
92–96 Marks are awarded here for verbs which are emphatic, appropriate and interesting. For example:
92 *stumbled*
93–94 *screamed, leap*
95 *wandered*
96 *shuddered*
97–100 Any sensible answers awarded marks here, for example: *podcast, hippy, television, grunge, software, nerd, jukebox, reggae, website, clone, hashtag.*

Paper 6 (pages 27–32)

1 **hill** The text states in line 5 that the train is 'pulling up Beattock, a steady climb'.
2 **to see what is making the noise** The text states in line 11 that the 'birds turn their heads as she approaches' because it has been 'snorting noisily' (line 9).
3 **ones with no windows** The type of mail coach the poet was writing about had no windows, as the interior walls were fitted out with pigeonholes into which the mail could be sorted while the train was moving – hence 'blank-faced coaches'.
4–6 *cheques, postal orders, letters (lines 2 and 3)*
7 *As the train moves forward the steam makes a trail over the 'shoulder' of the train.*
8 *goes downhill*
9 *Tall chimney stacks facing each other in rows.*

10 References to either 'In the farm she passes no one wakes' (line 15) or 'But a jug in a bedroom gently shakes' (line 16) would be acceptable.
11 **press**ure
12 **detect**ive
13 **black**en
14 re**cover**ed
15 **sign**ature
16 **fresh**ly
17 **swim**ming
18 un**help**ful
19 **we** A pronoun is a word that replaces a noun in a sentence.
20 **play** A verb is an action word.
21 **sad** An adjective is a word that describes a noun.
22 **quickly** An adverb is a word that describes a verb.
23 **aunt** A noun is a word for a person or thing.
24 **it** A pronoun is a word that replaces a noun in a sentence.
25 **teach** A verb is an action word.
26 **lesson** The lesson started at eleven o'clock. 'Lesson' means a class, while to 'lessen' means to decrease.
27 **groan** The man gave a groan as he lifted the weight. A 'groan' is a disgruntled moan, while 'grown' means to have increased in size.
28 **board** Dad said we must get a new ironing board. A 'board' is a flat surface / piece of material, while 'bored' means to feel weary and impatient.
29 **lone** The lone sailor had crossed the ocean. 'Lone' means alone/isolated, while 'loan' is a sum which can be lent or borrowed.
30 **stakes** The gardener put in stakes for the sweet peas to climb. 'Stakes' are strong wooden or metal posts, while 'steaks' are pieces of meat.
31 **to** Kang had to help his teacher. 'To' is part of the infinitive of the verb 'to help', while 'two' is the number after one.
32 **hour** Alice had an hour to wait. An 'hour' is sixty minutes, while 'our' means belonging to us.
33–39 A common noun is an object. A proper noun is a name, place or date. An abstract noun is a noun that is a thought or feeling. A collective noun is a noun used for a group.
33 **proper**
34 **collective**
35 **common**
36 **abstract**
37 **collective**
38 **proper**
39 **abstract**
40 **to be short of money**
41 **to get into trouble**

42 **to have a short sleep**

43 **to crawl on hands and knees**

44 **to ask for trouble**

45 **to take punishment without complaint**

46 **to be treated badly**

47–53 A conjunction is a joining word such as 'and' or 'but' that joins two clauses together. Sometimes there is more than one conjunction that makes sense when joining two clauses.

47 **although, until, so** She didn't see me although/until/so I waved at her.

48 **since, while** I have learned to swim since/while I have been at this school.

49 **until, although** I cannot reach my books until/although you have moved that parcel.

50 **but, while** David likes his tea very hot but/while Brygid doesn't like tea at all.

51 **because, since, while** I couldn't sing because/since/while I had a sore throat.

52 **so** Kerry has cut her finger so she will have to wash it.

53 **and** I am very keen on swimming and I like diving too.

54 **burglary** When adding the suffix 'ary' to a word ending in 'e', the 'e' is removed first.

55 **confectionary** The suffix 'ary' is added.

56 **jewellery** When adding the suffix 'ery' to the word 'jewel', the 'l' is doubled.

57 **momentary** The suffix 'ary' is added.

58 **slippery** When adding the suffix 'ery' to the word 'slip', the 'p' is doubled.

59 **dictionary** The suffix 'ary' is added.

60 **shrubbery** When adding the suffix 'ery' to the word 'shrub', the 'b' is doubled.

61 **boundary** The suffix 'ary' is added.

62–67 Helper verbs or auxiliary verbs (such as will, shall, may, might, is, can, or could) are used before main verbs to express the tense/mood. Ensure the helper verbs are in the tenses given.

62 The car **was** speeding down the valley.

63 The birds **are** flying high in the sky.

64 A chicken **is** pecking in the dirt.

65 Two speed-boats **were** racing out to sea.

66 The sheep **are** flocking together on the moor.

67 A frog **was** jumping about in our pond.

68–71 "Can I have some of your drink?" asked Karen.

72–78 "Are you up yet?" Jake's mum called. "It is time for school."

79 **phone**

80 **cycle** or **bike**

81 **exam**

82 **photo**

83 **hippo**

84 **maths**

85 *Nelson and his ship, the 'Victory'.*

86 *Richard Edmunds*

87 *Friday and Saturday*

88 *It will give them information about the historic ship moored at their city.* The headteacher 'would like to encourage people from the local area to come and watch as they might learn something new about the historic ship moored at their city.'.

89 Child's own heading showing evidence s/he has thought about what might attract the reader to read the article, e.g. *Barncroft Primary School to stage Nelson's Adventure*.

90–95 There are several options for these answers; marks are given for any correctly spelled words using the prefixes. Here are some suggestions:

90 *co-operate*

91 *re-enter*

92 *bi-monthly*

93 *cross-reference*

94 *de-ice*

95 *ex-directory*

96 She **will take** a photo.

97 I **will/shall wake** up at 7 o'clock.

98 I **will/shall enjoy** that piece of cake.

99 It **will rain**/it **will be** raining.

100 We **will play** on the swings.

Paper 7 (pages 33–37)

1 **It would give him food for three days** The text states in lines 1–2 that 'there was enough meat for three whole days'.

2 **rushed along shouting** The text states in lines 6–7 that 'the hyena's children rushed towards the village, shouting the news at the top of their voices'.

3–4 **the hyena, smaller wild animals** The hyena joined his children as 'he started off to join a band of other animals who were running towards the village' (lines 13–14) after seeing 'all the smaller wild animals [run] towards the village' (lines 8–9)

5 *They would quickly finish the meat he had found.* He knew their 'healthy young teeth and growing appetites' (line 3).

6 *No, he made it up to get rid of his children.*

7 *As animals heard the news they told friends and family and the message spread.*

8–9 *So many animals passed him on the way to the village that eventually the hyena thought that maybe he had been right and therefore headed to the village to find all the dead asses.* Evidence from passage needed to support answer, e.g. 'Well, he said to himself, it looks as if it must be true'.

10 **basement** The suffix 'ment' is added.

11 **happiness** The 'y' is removed and replaced with an 'i' before the suffix 'ness' is added.

12 **argument** The 'e' is removed before the suffix 'ment' is added.

13 **spiteful** The suffix 'ful' is added.

14 **useful** The suffix 'ful' is added.

15 **loneliness** The 'y' is removed and replaced with an 'i' before the suffix 'ness' is added.

16–21 An 'adjectival phrase' is a group of words that describe a noun or pronoun in a sentence thus functioning as an adjective.

16 The **hollow-eyed, pale-faced** mask frightened the children.

17 The **huge, mottled brown** horse bounded about the field.

18 Snow fell from the **twisted, broken** branch.

19 The **cold and fresh** water tasted lovely.

20 George put on his **warm, cosy** jumper.

21 The **long, smooth** snake hid under the rock for protection.

22 **Italy**

23 **Australia**

24 **China**

25 **France**

26 **America**

27 **India**

28–35 There are many possible answers for each question. Sensible answers will be given marks. For example:

28 *quietly, worriedly*

29 *angrily, loudly*

30 *loudly, rudely*

31 *well, soundly*

32 *softly, sorrowfully*

33 *smugly, cheekily*

34 *heartily, hysterically*

35 *sternly, crossly*

36–42 Commas are used to separate the main clause from a subordinate clause in a sentence. (See the answer to Paper 2 Q18–23 for more explanation.) They also surround any additional information.

36 Mark suddenly jumped, the dog having caught him unawares.

37–38 Time and time again, as the boat was tossed by the waves, the helicopter crew tried to save the fishermen.

39–40 The shop, which earlier had been bustling with shoppers, was now quiet.

41–42 Susie and Tariq, already soaked from the pouring rain, ran to find cover.

43–44 **richer richest**

45–46 **worse worst**

47–48 **quieter quietest**

49–50 **prettier prettiest**

51–52 **more most**

53–54 **earlier earliest**

55 **fork**

56 **fortnight**

57 **doorbell** or **knocker**

58 **recite** or **recount**

59 **puppet** or **marionette**

60 **stem** or **stalk**

61 **stage**

62 **string**

63–68 The spelling rule is to change the 'f' to 'v' and then add 'es'.

63 **halves**

64 **shelves**

65 **thieves**

66 **leaves**

67 **knives**

68 **calves**

69–87 "Quick!" shouted Nina. "The water will trap us in the cave if we don't hurry."
"I know!" screamed James, trying to be heard above the thundering waves.
As James ran, his feet barely touched the ground.

88 **pizza**

89 **volcano**

90 **piano**

91 **umbrella**

92 **Italy**

93 *ordinary* or *unattractive* or *simple*

94 *pull* or *drag* or *strain*

95 *force* or *persuade* or *poke* or *press*

96 **pull** 'Tug' means to pull or drag.

97–98 An ambulance **is** speeding to the accident as many people **are** hurt.

99 There **was** a party at Sonia's house.

100 Many children **were** enjoying the firework display.

Paper 8 (pages 37–42)

1 **Toad talks too much** The girl says 'you hurt my head' (line 8) because 'you talk too much'. (line 7)

2 **Thursday** Lines 11–12 tell us 'This is a Thursday'.

3–4 *He doesn't think very highly of them. He shows this when he says that he has 'several aunts who ought to be washerwomen' (line 6).*

5–6 *I would have felt angry because I was trying to help and he was being rude about my aunt.*

7 *Some words are put into italics to highlight the strength of feeling/importance that they hold in the text. They are used to indicate that those words are emphasised by the characters speaking them.*

8–10 *horrid – for speaking in an unflattering way*
about her aunt
proud – not willing to be seen as a washerwoman
ungrateful – for his reaction to her suggestion

11–12 *The washerwoman demanded that she should*
be bound, gagged and dumped in a corner
(line 37). This was to help persuade the guards
that she had nothing to do with Toad's escape.

13–22 Possible answers:

13–14 *pretty, attractive*

15–16 *wrong, incorrect*

17–18 *happy, amused*

19–20 *mean, unkind*

21–22 *shout, yell*

23 Tim **did** his homework.

24 Every boy **was** on the field.

25 They **are** late today.

26 All the men **were** working.

27 I **have** eaten all the cakes.

28 We **shall** take the dog for a walk.

29 I dropped the bag but not one of the eggs **has** broken.

30 They **will** collect the old bed.

31–38 The suffixes 'en', 'ise' and 'ify' added to a word change a noun into a verb. Several of the answers below have more than one option of suffixes to add.

31 **dramatise**

32 **solidify**

33 **magnetise** or **magnify**

34 **thicken**

35 **terrorise** or **terrify**

36 **weaken**

37 **blacken**

38 **fertilise**

39–43 There are several possible answers for some of the below. Marks are awarded for any words with the same *ough* sound, correctly spelled.

39 *fought, ought*

40 *borough*

41 *enough*

42 *bough*

43 *dough*

44–47 "When can we go swimming?" asked Jenny.

48–51 "We will be late!" Mum yelled.

52–55 A conjunction is a joining word such as 'and' or 'but' that joins two clauses together.

52 **where** The ship had called at many ports, finally arriving in Dublin where the sailors could go on leave.

53 **because** Wendy was soaking because she had fallen in the river.

54 **although** Daniel always found maths very difficult although he tried very hard.

55 **which** Mum bought a new jumper which came with a free skirt.

56–64 A quick way of remembering which word to use is that 'there' is connected to the words 'here' and 'where'. An apostrophe shows where there are missing letters in a contraction so 'they're' is a shortened form of 'they are'. 'Their' means 'belonging to them'.

56 **there** I would like to go there today.

57 **they're** They're waiting for the bus.

58 **their** I like the colour of their school uniform.

59 **there** "What a huge amount of work **there** is to do," sighed Mark.

60–61 **their, their** The children were told to put their books inside their bags.

62 **they're** They're very quiet.

63–64 **their, there** They put their coats over there.

65 **km**

66 **UK**

67 **CD**

68 **MP**

69 **USA**

70 **TV**

71 **Dr**

72–77 When using 'anything' or 'nothing' note that 'nothing' can not be used when there is already an existing negative phrase in the sentence (so as to avoid a double negative).

72 **anything** David didn't say anything as he travelled to school

73 **nothing** "There is nothing to do," moaned Tanya.

74 **anything** Nasar can't find anything in his messy room.

75 **anything** Sonia didn't have anything for breakfast.

76 **nothing** There is nothing to paint with.

77 **nothing** It is nothing to do with me!

78 **Ben asked where his bag was.**

79 **Dad said we needed to be quick.**

80 **The children asked whether they could go to the fair.**

81 **The teacher explained that they were going to bake a cake.**

82–87 Possible answers:

82 *empty*

83 *hung/hanging*

84 *vain/proud*

85 *finished*

86 *cruelly*

87 *understood*

88 **noun.**

89 **noun.**

90 **noun.**

91 **verb.**

92 **verb.**

93 **verb.**

94 **false** The text starts by saying 'No dogs in our playground' as a title.

95 **don't know** There is no mention of there being a slide in the playground.

96 **false** The text states that 'they frighten some children'.

97 **true** The text ends with saying 'please walk your dogs in the park area…'.

98 **false** The text suggests that dogs should not be in the playground regardless of whether or not their owners are present.

99 **false** The text states that 'they leave a mess'.

100 **true** The text states that dogs should be walked in the park area 'around the duck pond'.

Paper 9 (pages 43–47)

1 **sunny** Line 3 states that the narrator is sitting 'in steady heat' from the light of the 'level sun' (line 2).

2–3 **a farmer, me** The text states that 'A farmer snored' (line 5) and 'I leant against Mother and slept' (line 16).

4 'And gurgled awhile' (line 7)

5 'In the refreshment room.' Lines 10–11 tell us that this is 'the place where we changed...The refreshment room'.

6 'The last part of the journey home.'

7–8 The family have been to the sea, as indicated in line 12: 'And the salt on my face, not of tears, not tears, but the sea.'

9–10 As you read the poem the pace gets faster. The poet is trying to convey the speed of the train through the words he uses. We can see this through the constant use of commas and the long sentences.

11–12 When there is driving rain, the raindrops fall very fast and densely, making everything blurred and difficult to see. The poet is suggesting that the speed of the train is having the same effect on their view of the sights they are passing.

13–15 faster (line 1), charging (line 3), fly (line 6)

16 **flies** The spelling rule is to change the 'y' to 'ies' to make it plural.

17 **bullies** The spelling rule is to change the 'y' to 'ies' to make it plural.

18 **valleys** This word just needs an 's' added to make it plural.

19 **journeys** This word just needs an 's' added to make it plural.

20 **ladies** The spelling rule is to change the 'y' to 'ies' to make it plural.

21 **hobbies** The spelling rule is to change the 'y' to 'ies' to make it plural.

22 **cries** The spelling rule is to change the 'y' to 'ies' to make it plural.

23 **donkeys** This word just needs an 's' added to make it plural.

24–29 The prepositions here are used to describe the position or cause.

24 **up** He ran up the stairs.

25 **with** The teacher was cross with the cheeky boy.

26 **from** Your t-shirt is different from mine.

27 **over/up** The boy climbed over/up the wall.

28 **behind** The mouse hid behind the bush.

29 **on/behind** Dad hid the present on/behind the cupboard.

30 **Rosie's knitting was finished at last.** The apostrophe here indicates possession; that the knitting belongs to Rosie, and therefore it follows the name 'Rosie'.

31 **Tony's dog ran away last week.** The apostrophe here indicates possession; that the dog belongs to Tony, and therefore it follows the name 'Tony'.

32 **The two boys' football went over the fence.** There is more than one boy, so the apostrophe goes after the 's'.

33 **The three rabbits' hutches fell down in the wind.** There is more than one rabbit, so the apostrophe goes after the 's'.

34 **Caroline's leg hurt after she slopped on the ice.** The apostrophe here indicates possession; that the leg belongs to Caroline, and therefore it follows the name 'Caroline'.

35 **My mother's bedroom was a mess.** The apostrophe here indicates possession; that the bedroom belongs to the mother, and therefore it follows the name 'my mother'.

36–43 There are many possible examples for each spelling pattern. Here are a few examples:

36 *fight*
37 *dove*
38 *ridge*
39 *full*
40 *toast*
41 *more*
42 *strange*
43 *stitch*

44–52

	er	est	ish
long	longer	longest	longish
small	smaller	smallest	smallish
late	later	latest	latish

Because 'late' ends in an 'e' the spelling rule is to remove the 'e' before adding the 'er', 'est' and 'ish' endings.

53 **nothing**
54 **eat**
55 **little**

56 **yes**
57 **child**
58 **potatoes**
59 **headache**
60–62 The candles blew out, plunging the children into darkness.
63–65 Carrying piles of apples, the carts were pulled down the road.
66–68 High in the sky, the birds were feeding on the flying insects.
69–75 An abbreviation is a word that has been shortened after some letters are removed. An acronym is formed from the initial letters of a title or phrase.
    69 **UN**
    70 **BBC**
    71 **RAF**
    72 **NATO**
    73 **JP**
    74 **HGV**
    75 **CID**
76–87 A noun is word for an item, place or name. An adjective is a describing word. A verb is an action word. An adverb describes a verb. A preposition is a word to link nouns, pronouns, or phrases to other words in a sentence. Conjunctions connect clauses or sentences.
Nouns: *rabbit, cave, food, rock, remains, turnip, search*
Adjectives: *small, weak, mouldy*
Verbs: *searched, looking, could, find, were, sighed, continued*
Adverbs: *frantically, loudly*
Prepositions: *in, for, behind, of*
Conjunctions: *but, and*
88–91 Possible answers include: w*rite, raspberry,* p*salm, scissors*
    92 **He/She strokes** the dog.
    93 **He/She cries** loudly.
    94 **He/She washes his/her** hair.
    95 **He/She cooks** a meal.
    96 **drake**
    97 **actor**
    98 **prince**
    99 **hero**
  100 **landlord**

Paper 10 (pages 48–52)

1 **night-time** The passage starts by telling us that Sophie is 'In the moonlight'. (Line 1)
2 **as sharp as a knife** Line 2 states that his nose was 'sharp as a knife'.
3 **into her bed** Line 6 states that Sophie 'jumped into her bed'.

4–5 'devilish' – *the look of the devil, frightening* 'crouched' – *bending low, holding arms and legs together tightly*
6 *She was so scared she couldn't produce a sound.*
7–8 Possible answers include: *enormous, long, pale, wrinkly (lines 1 and 26–27)*
9–10 *'If you can think of anything more terrifying that that happening to you in the middle of the night, then let's hear about it.' (lines 23–24)* The author communicates with the reader like this to encourage us to put ourselves in Sophie's position and understand just how scary the situation is for Sophie.
11–12 *He is very large with a long, pale, wrinkly face. He has bright, flashing eyes, huge ears, a sharp nose, strong fingers, arms as thick as tree trunks and huge hands.*
13–15 Reference needs to be made to specific lines/phrases from the passage, e.g. *I think Sophie was terrified because she 'knew exactly what was going on although she couldn't see it happening'. The text states that 'a Monster... had plucked her from her bed in the witching hour', which must be very frightening.*
  16 **shyly** Just add 'ly'
  17 **spied** The spelling rule is to change 'y' to 'i' and then add 'ed'.
  18 **tried** The spelling rule is to change 'y' to 'i' and then add 'ed'.
  19 **easier** The spelling rule is to remove the 'y' and then add 'ier'.
  20 **drying** Just add 'ing'
  21 **cried** The spelling rule is to change 'y' to 'i' and then add 'ed'.
22–31 Capital letters are needed at the beginning of a sentence and for proper nouns (the name of a person, place or thing). Words such as 'of' and 'the' within a title do not need to be capitalised. **Suddenly,** out of the tunnel emerged the **Flying Scotsman. Hannah** and **Leroy** had been waiting for this moment, ever since reading about this train in **Famous Trains** of the **Past. They** screamed with excitement as it flew past them on its way to **Banbury.**
32–33 There are several possible options for these; any sensible words spelt correctly will be given a mark.
32–33 *everyone everything*
34–35 *candlelight candlestick*
36–37 *rainbow raindrop*
38–39 *playtime playground*
40–42 Each of the listed adverbs should be written in a sentence.
  40 *Barney shouted angrily at the bullies.*
  41 *The clown stupidly fell over.*

42 *The sun came out unexpectedly.*

43–54

Common nouns	Proper nouns	Collective nouns	Abstract nouns
door	France	team	love
leg	Nigel	bunch	sympathy
camel	Hyde Park	swarm	justice

55–60 The rule is to add '-cial' when the root word ends in 'ce'; if it ends in a consonant, remove the consonant and add '-tial'.

55 **cial** official (office)
56 **tial** confidential (confident)
57 **tial** essential (essence)
58 **cial** commercial (commerce)
59 **cial** artificial (artifice)
60 **tial** partial (part)

61–64 Any sensible adjectival phrases added in the gaps of sentences will have marks awarded.

61 *Tola slept peacefully in her cosy, warm bed.*
62 *The whooshing, shrieking fireworks went high in the sky.*
63 *Alice clutched her beloved, battered pale blue teddy.*
64 *Monty, the eight-year-old rescue dog, bounded through the long grass.*

65–72 A prefix is a group of letters added to the beginning of a root word to make a new, sensible word. Common prefixes include 're', 'di', 'dis', 'in', 'im', 'il' and 'un'. Here are some possible answers.

65 *deactivate, reactivate*
66 *rejoin, conjoin*
67 *mistreat, retreat*
68 *disembark*
69 *discontinue*
70 *redefine*
71 *decompose*
72 *overhead*

73 ✗ The correct spelling is 'shriek'. The spelling follows the 'i before e' spelling rule.
74 ✓
75 ✓
76 ✗ The correct spelling is 'receive'. The spelling follows the 'i before e' spelling rule.
77 ✗ The correct spelling is 'neigh'. The spelling is an exception to the 'i before e' spelling rule.
78 ✓
79 ✗ The correct spelling is 'siege'. The spelling follows the 'i before e' spelling rule.

80–85 A clause is a group of words that includes a subject and a verb. In each of the below there are two clauses to be underlined. The clauses are often separated by commas or conjunctions. In subordinate clauses the conjunction (e.g. because, while, as, although) is considered part of the clause, so can be underlined too. Where two main clauses are joined by a conjunction (e.g. and, but), the conjunction isn't considered part of the clause, so does not have to be underlined.

80–81 **Aden ran with all his might when he saw the raging bull.**
82–83 **Julie combed her hair constantly because she wanted straight hair.**
84–85 **While Yan was painting a picture, the lights suddenly went off.**

86–91 A parenthesis is a piece of additional information inserted into a sentence. It has a bracket/dash/comma before and after it. Possible answers are:

86–87 *Lula (who was Amy's best friend) had other ideas.*
88–89 *The cat – who was always sleeping – lazily stretched in the sunlight.*
90–91 *The suburb of Ealing, in west London, was home to the Khalid family.*

92–100 There are many words that can be used and make sense, but here are some that might be covered:

92–94 *whoosh, bang, zoom*
95–97 *plip plop, squelch, splash*
98–100 *moo, crunch, squeak*

Paper 11 (pages 53–57)

1 **disappear quickly and quietly** The text states in lines 5–6 that 'they disappear quickly and quietly when large stupid folk like you and me come blundering along'

2 **people** The text states in lines 5–7 that 'large stupid folk like you and me come blundering along, making a noise like elephants which they can hear a mile off.'

3 **brown** 'long brown fingers' (line 10)

4 *It enables them to hear people a mile away. (lines 6–7)*

5–6 *Their feet grow natural leather soles and they are covered in thick warm brown hair. (lines 8–9)*

7 *'...laugh deep fruity laughs especially after dinner which they have twice a day when they can get it.' (lines 10–11) This shows that they enjoy their food so much they have two dinners when they can, instead of just one!*

8 Main text should be line 10, not line 9–10

9–11 *Hobbits are half the size; Hobbits aren't stupid like the Big People; Hobbits have feet that grow natural leather soles and thick warm brown hair.*

12–14 *A possible answer could be: I think that the Big People are frightening because they are twice as tall as we are, so when they come near, I run away and hide. They are also quite stupid because they walk so heavily that we know they are coming.* Marks removed if not written in first person.

15–23 Words which are not homophones: **diner, dinner, bath, bathe, sit, thorough, pasted, lung, lunge.**

(The homophones listed are 'vein', 'vane' and 'vain'; 'cite', 'sight' and 'site'; 'through' and 'threw'; 'reign', 'rein' and 'rain'; 'passed' and 'past'; 'grisly' and 'grizzly'; and 'missed' and 'mist'.)

24 **sky** In the plural the 'y' is changed to an 'i' before 'es' is added.

25 **life** In the plural the 'f' is changed to a 'v' before 'es' is added.

26 **lorry** In the plural the 'y' is changed to an 'i' before 'es' is added.

27 **giraffe** To make the plural, add an 's'.

28 **ox** To make the plural, add 'en'.

29 **posy** In the plural the 'y' is changed to an 'i' before 'es' is added.

30–35 Three sentences, each sentence including two possessive pronouns underlined. For example: *Ours* is bigger than *his*. A possessive pronoun is a pronoun showing to whom something belongs. For example, words such as mine, ours, his, hers, yours and theirs are possessive pronouns.

36–41 Sometimes there is more than one conjunction that makes sense when joining two clauses.

36 **but** The rain poured in through the window but no one noticed.

37 **but, although** I knew where my toothbrush should be but/although I couldn't find it.

38 **until** The dog scratched at the door until someone let him in.

39 **when** I like fish and chips when I am feeling hungry.

40 **and** Sheena loves reading and also writing stories.

41 **but, although** Deano was tired but/although he didn't want to go to bed.

42–49 A prefix is a group of letters that can be added to the beginning of a root word to make a new, sensible word. The given prefixes here are 'bi' which means 'two', 'circum' which means 'around', 'auto' which means 'self', and 'tele' which means 'over distance'. There is only one possible prefix for each answer below.

42 **tele** telephone

43 **auto** automotive

44 **circum** circumnavigate

45 **bi** biplane

46 **tele** television

47 **auto** autobiography

48 **tele** telescope

49 **bi** bifocals

50–67 Nouns: **coffee, horror, scoundrel**
Verbs: **jumped, threw, going**
Adjectives: **strange, curly, thin**
Adverbs: **truly, really, almost**
Prepositions: **of, into, with**
Pronouns: **it, himself, you**

68–73 'Was' is used in the first person singular (I) and in the third person singular (he, she, it) whereas 'were' is used in the second person singular (you, your, yours) and first and third person plural (we, they).

68–69 **were, was** They were ready to go swimming but the pool was not open.

70 **were** All the children had finished their lunch and were ready to go out to the play.

71–72 **were, was** They were queuing for hours as the film was supposed to be brilliant.

73 **was** Sam wondered whether it was time to get up.

74–80 The below are well-known expressions.

74 **to hang your head**

75 **to be a wet blanket**

76 **to turn over a new leaf**

77 **to take a back seat**

78 **to put the cart before the horse**

79 **to smell a rat**

80 **to sit on the fence**

81–84 Amusing sentences containing the given preposition e.g. *It was only after leaning against the fence that Josh realised it had just been painted.* A preposition is a word used to link nouns, pronouns or phrases to other words within a sentence. They act to connect the people, objects, time and locations of a sentence. For example: for, of, before, after, between.

85–92

France	Spain	Italy
café	tortilla	gondola
boutique	mosquito	macaroni
adieu	armadillo	opera

93–100 A contraction is when two words are merged together, with one or more of the letters removed. An apostrophe is used to show where letters have been removed.

93 **we'll**

94 **they'll**

95 **shouldn't**

96 **I've**

97 **hasn't**

98 **won't**

99 **there's**

100 **you're**

Bond English Assessment Papers 9–10 years Book 1

1 **India** Line 1 states that Delhi is 'the capital of India'.

2 **people** Line 5 states that the king is worried that the snake-god could bring 'fire and plague to his subjects' and that he therefore ordered them to 'offer prayers and sacrifices to placate the snake-god' which suggests that they are the people in his land.

3 **six hundred years ago** Line 10 states that the tower was built 'about six hundred years ago'.

4 *as hard as he could*

5–6 *'The king trembled at the thought of the snake-god's anger – would he bring fire and plague to his subjects, or even destroy the world?'*

7 Possible answers include: *gifts, offerings*

8–9 *I would have felt upset because I had just put my kingdom and all of my subjects in danger.*

10–11 *No more war and unrest*

12–19 Adding the prefix 'in' or 'im' turns the word into the negative version of itself. There is only one possible answer for each of the below.

12 **im** imperfect   13 **in** incorrect
14 **in** inaccurate   15 **im** impure
16 **Im** imbalance   17 **in** incomplete
18 **im** impatient   19 **in** invisible

20 **Mum called that it was time for dinner.**

21 **The children asked if they could go out to play.**

22 **David whispered to Amie that he was hiding in the shed.**

23 **The postman mumbled that it was really cold today.**

24 **Gina exclaimed that she loved her new shoes.**

25–31 There are many words that can be used and make sense, but here are some that might be covered:

25 *crackle*
26 *gasp, pant*   27 *squelch*
28 *thump*   29 *slam*
30 *splash*   31 *beep, beep*

32 **fitted** The consonant 't' is doubled before the suffix 'ed' is added.

33 **carried** The 'y' is changed to 'i' before the suffix 'ed' is added.

34 **knotted** The consonant 't' is doubled before the suffix 'ed' is added.

35 **picked** Just add the suffix 'ed'.

36 **married** The 'y' is changed to 'i' before the suffix 'ed' is added.

37 **hunted** Just add the suffix 'ed'.

38–41 To turn the below two sentences into a single sentence add a conjunction between the two sentences instead of the existing full stop.

38 *Tom ate his food because he was very hungry.*

39 *The sun shone brightly and woke Gemma up.*

40 *The school trip was great fun and they didn't want to go home.*

41 *Nasar learnt his spelling homework but he still got some wrong in the test.*

42 **past** The word 'licked' show that the action took place in the past.

43 **past** The words 'was swimming' show that the action took place in the past.

44 **present** The words 'is sleeping' show that the action takes place in the present.

45 **present** The words 'is laying' show that the action takes place in the present.

46 **future** The words 'shall not' show that the action takes place in the future.

47 **past** The word 'ate' shows that the action took place in the past.

48 **future** The words 'will go' shows that the action takes place in the future.

49–60 Nouns: **beauty, bread**
Adjectives: **silky, fluffy**
Verbs: **stumbled, heaved**
Adverbs: **frantically, stupidly**
Prepositions: **of, among**
Conjunctions: **because, although**

61–68 The answer should be a word that has the same meaning as the word in bold in the sentence. Here are some possible answers:

61 *tried*   62 *asked*
63 *said*   64 *stuck*
65 *often*   66 *given*
67 *rich*   68 *clapped*

69–74 An abstract noun is a thought, feeling or idea. The suffixes can be removed to form verbs. The correct verbs are listed below.

69 **attract**
70 **entertain**   71 **depart**
72 **attach**   73 **fail**
74 **complete**   75 **away**
76 **clock**   77 **makes**
78 **fill**   79 **drain**
80 **stair**   81 **same**

82–85 Double negatives are two negative words used in the same sentence. Using two negatives turns the sentence into a positive one (which is confusing).

82 **I haven't got any money. / I have no money.**

83 **There wasn't a clown at the circus. / There were no clowns at the circus.**

84 **There weren't any sweets in the jar. / There were no sweets in the jar.**

85 **Tina hasn't got an umbrella for the rain. / Tina has no umbrella for the rain.**

86–100 "Quick, come here!" called Tom.
The rain was falling heavily and they wanted to avoid getting wet.
"When do you think it will stop?" asked Misha.

Barncroft Primary School, Portsmouth, is putting on a play, *Nelson's Adventures*, portraying the adventures of Nelson in his flagship, the *Victory*. The whole school has worked on this drama project for the last week after visiting the ship. Richard Edmunds, who plays Nelson, is reported to have said that it has been the best week at school he has ever had.

The children are performing to the general public on Friday 4th and Saturday 5th November at 7.30 p.m. Mrs Danielle Turnpike, the headteacher, would like to encourage people from the local area to come and watch as they might learn something new about the historic ship moored at their city. All the money the performances earn will be given to 'Children in Need'.

Read the newspaper article and answer the questions.

85 Barncroft Primary School is putting on a play. What is it about?

_____

86 Who is playing Nelson?

_____

87 On what days of the week are the performances?

_____

88 Why will the play be particularly interesting to the people of Portsmouth?

_____

89 This newspaper article is missing a heading. Write your own heading for this article.

_____

5

Write a hyphenated word using each prefix.

90 co _____

91 re _____

92 bi _____

93 cross _____

94 de _____

95 ex _____

6

Rewrite these sentences in the **future tense**.

96 She took a photo.

_____

97 I woke up at 7 o'clock.

_____

98 I enjoyed that piece of cake.

_____

99 It is raining.

_____

100 We played on the swings.

_____

5

Now go to the Progress Chart to record your score!   Total   100

The hyena once had the luck to come upon a dead ass. There was enough meat for
three whole days. He was busy enjoying his meal when suddenly he saw his children
coming. He knew their healthy young teeth and growing appetites, and as he did not
want to share the magnificent carcass with them, he said: "You see that village over
there? If you're quick you'll find plenty of asses there, just like this one. Only run." 5

The hyena's children rushed towards the village, shouting the news at the top of
their voices. As the tale travelled to all corners of the bush, starving animals crept
out – jackals, civet-cats, tiger-cats – all the smaller wild animals ran towards the
village where the feast of asses' meat was to be found.

The whole morning the hyena watched them go by, singly or in flocks, until in 10
the end he began to be worried.

Well, he said to himself, it looks as if it must be true. That village must be full of
dead asses. And leaving the carcass he had had all to himself, he started off to join
a band of other animals who were running towards the village.

The Hyena and the Dead Ass a West African tale retold by René Guillot

Underline the correct answers.

1 Why was the hyena lucky to find a dead ass?

(It would keep him warm at night,

It would feed his family,

It would give him food for three days)

2 What did the hyena's children do on their way to the village?

(crept along quietly, rushed along shouting, crept along shouting)

3–4 Who joined the hyena's children at the village?

(asses, only jackals, the hyena, smaller wild animals)

Answer these questions.

5 Why didn't the hyena want his children to eat with him?

_____

6 Were there plenty of dead asses at the village? Explain your answer.

_____

7 How do you think the tale of the dead asses travelled to the corners of the bush?

_____

8–9 Why do you think the hyena joined the other animals in running towards the village? Include a line from the text to support your answer.

_____

_____

_____

5

E 2

Add the **suffix** to each of these words. Make any spelling changes necessary.

10 base + ment _____ **11** happy + ness _____

12 argue + ment _____ **13** spite + ful _____

14 use + ful _____ **15** lonely + ness _____

6

D 6

Underline the **adjectival phrase** in each sentence.

16 The hollow-eyed, pale-faced mask frightened the children.

17 The huge, mottled brown horse bounded about the field.

18 Snow fell from the twisted, broken branch.

19 The cold and fresh water tasted lovely.

20 George put on his warm, cosy jumper.

21 The long, smooth snake hid under the rock for protection.

6

E 2

With a line match the country from where you think each word is borrowed.

22 pasta   Australia

23 boomerang   China

24 wok   Italy

25 restaurant   America

26 moose   India

27 pyjamas   France

6

Complete each sentence using a different **adverb**.

28 I whispered _____.

29 We shouted _____.

30 I coughed _____.

31 We slept _____.

32 I cried _____.

33 We chuckled _____.

34 I laughed _____.

35 We argued _____.

Add the missing commas to these sentences.

36 Mark suddenly jumped the dog having caught him unawares.

37–38 Time and time again as the boat was tossed by the waves the helicopter crew tried to save the fishermen.

39–40 The shop which earlier had been bustling with shoppers was now quiet.

41–42 Susie and Tariq already soaked from the pouring rain ran to find cover.

Complete the following **adjectives** of comparison.

Example: good   *better*   *best*

43–44 rich   _____   _____

45–46 bad   _____   _____

47–48 quiet   _____   _____

49–50 pretty   _____   _____

51–52 many   _____   _____

53–54 early   _____   _____

Give one word for each of these **definitions**.

55 Can be used when eating. It has three or four prongs set on the end of a handle.   _____

56 A period of two weeks.   _____

57 A door fitting which makes a noise to attract the attention of someone inside.   _____

58 To say something aloud from memory.   _____

59 A doll worked by pulling wires or strings in a toy theatre.   _____

60 The long, vertical part of a plant that supports the leaves and flowers.   _____

61 A raised platform on which plays are often performed. _____

62 Thin rope, line or cord used for tying up parcels. _____

Write each of these words in their **plural** form.

63 half _____ **64** shelf _____

65 thief _____ **66** leaf _____

67 knife _____ **68** calf _____

Copy the passage, adding the missing capital letters and punctuation.

69–87 quick shouted nina the water will trap us in the cave if we don't hurry
I know screamed james trying to be heard above the thundering waves
as james ran his feet barely touched the ground

_____

_____

_____

_____

_____

Write a word to match each picture.

88

_____

89

_____

90

_____

91

_____

92 All the words in questions 88–91 originate from the same country.

Which country is it? _____

8
E 2
6
D 4
D 5
19
E 2
4
E 2
1

pick	choice, choose, gather
piece	bit, chip, part, splinter, slice
pile	heap, collection, stack
plain	ordinary, unattractive, simple
pull	drag, tow, strain
push	force, persuade, poke, press

93 Write a word that has a similar meaning to 'plain'.   _____

94 Write a word that has a similar meaning to 'tow'.   _____

95 Write a synonym for the word 'push'.   _____

96 Next to which word in bold would you put
   the word 'tug'?   _____   (4)

Underline the correct word in brackets.

97–98 An ambulance (is, are) speeding to the accident as many people (is, are) hurt.

99 There (was, were) a party at Sonia's house.

100 Many children (was, were) enjoying the firework display.   (4)

Now go to the Progress Chart to record your score!   **Total** (100)

Paper 8

One morning the girl was very thoughtful, and answered at random, and did not seem
to Toad to be paying proper attention to his witty sayings and sparkling comments.
   'Toad,' she said presently, 'just listen, please. I have an aunt who is a
washerwoman.'
   'There, there,' said Toad graciously and affably, 'never mind; think no more about   5
it. *I* have several aunts who *ought* to be washerwomen.'
   'Do be quiet a minute, Toad,' said the girl. 'You talk too much, that's your chief
fault, and I'm trying to think, and you hurt my head. As I said, I have an aunt who
is a washerwoman; she does washing for all the prisoners in this castle – we try to
keep any paying business of that sort in the family, you understand. She takes   10
out the washing on Monday morning, and brings it in on Friday evening. This is a
Thursday. Now, this is what occurs to me: you're very rich – at least you're always
telling me so – and she's very poor. A few pounds wouldn't make any difference to
you, and it would mean a lot to her. Now, I think if she were properly approached
– squared, I believe, is the word you animals use – you could come to some   15

(37)

arrangement by which she would let you have her dress and bonnet and so on, and you could escape from the castle as the official washerwoman. You're very alike in many respects – particularly about the figure.'

'We're *not*,' said the Toad in a huff. 'I have a very elegant figure – for what I am.'

'So has my aunt,' replied the girl, 'for what *she* is. But have it your own way. You horrid, proud ungrateful animal, when I'm sorry for you, and trying to help you!' 20

'Yes, yes, that's all right; thank you very much indeed,' said the Toad hurriedly. 'But look here! you wouldn't surely have Mr. Toad, of Toad Hall, going about the country disguised as a washerwoman!'

'Then you can stop here as a Toad,' replied the girl with much spirit. 'I suppose you want to go off in a coach-and-four!' 25

Honest Toad was always ready to admit himself in the wrong. 'You are a good, kind, clever girl,' he said, 'and I am indeed a proud and stupid toad. Introduce me to your worthy aunt, if you will be so kind, and I have no doubt that the excellent lady and I will be able to arrange terms satisfactory to both parties.' 30

Next evening the girl ushered her aunt into Toad's cell, bearing his week's washing pinned up in a towel. The old lady had been prepared beforehand for the interview, and the sight of certain gold sovereigns that Toad had thoughtfully placed on the table in full view practically completed the matter and left little further to discuss. In return for his cash, Toad received a cotton print gown, an apron, a 35 shawl, and a rusty black bonnet; the only stipulation the old lady made being that she should be gagged and bound and dumped down in a corner.

From *The Wind in the Willows* by Kenneth Grahame

Underline the correct answers.

1 Why does the girl say her head hurts?

(she knocks it, Toad talks too much, Toad upset her)

2 What day of the week is it at the beginning of this passage?

(Monday, Thursday, Friday)

2

Answer these questions.

3–4 How does Toad feel about washerwomen in the beginning of the story? Pick out one piece of evidence to support your view.

_____

_____

5–6 Describe in your own words how you would have felt about Toad's reaction to the suggestion that he escapes the castle as a washerwoman, if you were the girl.

_____

_____

7 Why are some of the words in the passage written in *italics*?

_____

5

8–10 The girl describes Toad as a 'horrid, proud and ungrateful animal' (line 21). Why do you think she used each of these **adjectives**?

_____

_____

_____

11–12 What was the washerwoman's only demand and why do you think she made it?

_____

_____

Write two **antonyms** for each word.

13–14 ugly   _____   _____

15–16 right   _____   _____

17–18 sad   _____   _____

19–20 kind   _____   _____

21–22 whisper   _____   _____

Underline the correct word in the brackets.

23 Tim (done, did) his homework.

24 Every boy (were, was) on the field.

25 They (are, was) late today.

26 All the men (were, was) working.

27 I (have, shall) eaten all the cakes.

28 We (have, shall) take the dog for a walk.

29 I dropped the bag but not one of the eggs (has, shall) broken.

30 They (will, were) collect the old bed.

Change these words into verbs by adding _en_, _ise_ or _ify_.

31 drama   _____   **32** solid   _____

33 magnet   _____   **34** thick   _____

35 terror   _____   **36** weak   _____

37 black   _____   **38** fertile   _____

Next to each word write another word with the same *ough* sound.

39 bought   _____   40 thorough   _____

41 rough   _____   42 plough   _____

43 though   _____.

D 6
5
D 5

Rewrite these sentences and add the missing punctuation.

44–47 When can we go swimming asked Jenny

_____

48–51 We will be late Mum yelled

_____

8
D 2

In each gap add a **connective**.

    although   where   because   which

52 The ship had called at many ports, finally arriving in Dublin _____ the sailors could go on leave.

53 Wendy was soaking _____ she had fallen in the river.

54 Daniel always found maths very difficult _____ he tried very hard.

55 Mum bought a new jumper _____ came with a free skirt.

4
E 2

Write *there, their* or *they're* in each of the gaps. Don't forget capital letters, if necessary.

56 I would like to go _____ today.

57 _____ waiting for the bus.

58 I like the colour of _____ school uniform.

59 "What a huge amount of work _____ is to do," sighed Mark.

60–61 The children were told to put _____ books inside _____ bags.

62 _____ very quiet!

63–64 They put _____ coats over _____.

9
D 10

Write the **abbreviations** of these words.

65 kilometre   _____

66 United Kingdom   _____

67 compact disc   _____

68 Member of Parliament _____

69 United States of America _____

70 television _____

71 Doctor _____

Add *anything* or *nothing* to each of these sentences.

72 David didn't say _____ as he travelled to school.

73 "There is _____ to do," moaned Tanya.

74 Nasar can't find _____ in his messy room.

75 Sonia didn't have _____ for breakfast.

76 There is _____ to paint with.

77 It is _____ to do with me!

Rewrite these sentences as **reported speech**.

78 "Where is my bag?" asked Ben.

_____

79 "We need to be quick," said Dad.

_____

80 "Can we go to the fair?" asked the children.

_____

81 "We are going to bake a cake," the teacher explained.

_____

Write a **synonym** for the word in bold.

82 The house was **vacant** for some time. _____

83 It was **suspended** from the ceiling. _____

84 The girl was very **conceited**. _____

85 Michael had **completed** his work. _____

86 He treated the horse **brutally**. _____

87 She **comprehended** what the man said. _____

7

D 6

6

D 12

4

D 9

6

Write whether each word is a **noun** or a **verb**.

Example: inform   *verb*

88 suggestion   _____

89 cloudiness   _____

90 conservation   _____

91 discuss   _____

92 insulate   _____

93 specialise   _____

D 6

6

B

NO DOGS IN OUR PLAYGROUND

Keep dogs away from our playground because ...

❏ they frighten some children

❏ they get in the way of the swings

❏ they leave a mess

Please walk your dogs in the park area around the duck pond.

Write *true*, *false* or *don't know* next to each statement.

94 Dogs are allowed in the playground.   _____

95 There is a slide in the playground.   _____

96 Dogs frighten all children.   _____

97 Dogs should be walked in the park area.   _____

98 Dogs can be in the playground if they are with their owners.   _____

99 Dogs never leave a mess.   _____

100 The park has a duck pond.   _____

7

Now go to the Progress Chart to record your score!   Total   100

Paper 9

Journey Home

I remember the long homeward ride, begun
By the light that slanted in from the level sun;
And on the far embankment, in sunny heat,
Our whole train's shadow travelling dark and complete.
A farmer snored. Two loud gentlemen spoke   5
Of the cricket and news. The pink baby awoke
And gurgled awhile. Till slowly out of the day
The last light sank in glimmer and ash-grey.
I remember it all; and dimly remember, too,
The place where we changed – the dark trains lumbering through;   10
The refreshment room, the crumbs, and the slopped tea;
And the salt on my face, not of tears, not tears, but the sea.
"Our train at last!" said Father. "Now tumble in!
It's the last lap home!" And I wondered what 'lap' could mean;
But the rest is all lost, for a huge drowsiness crept   15
Like a yawn upon me; I leant against Mother and slept.

by John Walsh

Underline the correct answers.

  1 The weather was (cold, stormy, sunny, grey).

  2–3 In the poem two people and the baby slept. Who were they?

   (a gentleman, a farmer, me).   3

Answer these questions.

  4 What words show that the baby might be happy?

  _____

  5 Where did the family wait for their second train?

  _____

  6 What do you think 'the last lap home' means? (line 14)

  _____

  7–8 Where have the family been? Copy a line from the poem to support your answer.

  _____

  _____   5

Now read the first verse of *From a Railway Carriage* by R L Stevenson.

Faster than fairies, faster than witches,
Bridges and houses, hedges and ditches;
And charging along like troops in a battle,
All through the meadows the horses and cattle;
All of the sights of the hill and the plain   5
Fly as thick as driving rain;
And ever again, in the wink of an eye,
Painted stations whistle by.

9–10 This poem was also written about a train journey. What do you notice about the pace of this poem? What is the pace trying to convey to the reader?

_____

_____ ◯ 2

In your own words describe what is meant by:

11–12 'All of the sights of the hill and the plain
Fly as thick as driving rain;' (lines 5–6)

_____

_____ ◯ 2

13–15 Find three different words that highlight the speed at which the train is moving.

_____ (line _____)

_____ (line _____)

_____ (line _____) ◯ 3

◻ E 2

Write each of these words in its **plural form**.

16 fly	_____	**17** bully	_____
18 valley	_____	**19** journey	_____
20 lady	_____	**21** hobby	_____
22 cry	_____	**23** donkey	_____

◯ 8

Write a suitable **preposition** in each gap.

on   with   behind   over   from   up

24 He ran _____ the stairs.

25 The teacher was cross _____ the cheeky boy.

26 Your t-shirt is different _____ mine.

27 The boy climbed _____ the wall.

28 The mouse hid _____ the bush.

29 Dad hid the present _____ the cupboard.

6

Rewrite these sentences, adding the missing apostrophes.

30 Rosies knitting was finished at last.

_____

31 Tonys dog ran away last week.

_____

32 The two boys football went over the fence.

_____

33 The three rabbits hutches fell down in the wind.

_____

34 Carolines leg hurt after she slipped on the ice.

_____

35 My mothers bedroom was a mess.

6

_____

Next to each word write another word with the same spelling pattern.

36 light   _____   37 love   _____

38 bridge   _____   39 bull   _____

40 boast   _____   41 core   _____

42 range   _____   43 ditch   _____

8

Complete the table below.

44–52

	er	est	ish
long			
small			
late			

With a line match the **dialect** words with their meaning.

53 nowt	eat
54 scoff	potatoes
55 wee	child
56 aye	yes
57 bairn	headache
58 tatties	nothing
59 skullache	little

Copy these sentences and add the missing punctuation and capital letters.

60–62 the candles blew out plunging the children into darkness

_____

63–65 carrying piles of apples the carts were pulled down the road

_____

66–68 high in the sky the birds were feeding on the flying insects

_____

Abbreviate these words into their **abbreviations** or **acronyms**.

69 United Nations _____

70 British Broadcasting Corporation _____

71 Royal Air Force _____

72 North Atlantic Treaty Organisation _____

73 Justice of the Peace _____

74 Heavy Goods Vehicle _____

75 Criminal Investigation Department _____

Use words from the passage to complete the table.

> The small, weak rabbit searched frantically in the cave looking for food but all it could find behind a rock were the remains of a mouldy turnip. The rabbit sighed loudly and continued the search.

76–87

Noun	Adjective	Verb	Adverb	Preposition	Conjunction

12

Write four words with a silent letter.

E 2

88 _____   89 _____

90 _____   91 _____

4

Rewrite each sentence as though you are writing about someone else.

D 6

     Example: I feel cold. *She feels cold.*

92 I stroke the dog.   _____

93 I cry loudly.   _____

94 I wash my hair.   _____

95 I cook a meal.   _____

4

Write the masculine form of each of these words.

D 8

96 duck   _____   97 actress   _____

98 princess   _____   99 heroine   _____

100 landlady   _____

5

Now go to the Progress Chart to record your score!   Total   100

47

In the moonlight, Sophie caught a glimpse of an enormous long pale wrinkly face with the most enormous ears. The nose was as sharp as a knife, and above the nose there were two bright flashing eyes, and the eyes were staring straight at Sophie. There was a fierce and devilish look about them.

Sophie gave a yelp and pulled back from the window. She flew across the dormitory and jumped into her bed and hid under the blanket.   5

And there she crouched, still as a mouse, and tingling all over.

Under the blanket Sophie waited.

After a minute or so, she lifted a corner of the blanket and peeped out.

For the second time that night her blood froze to ice and she wanted to scream,   10
but no sound came out. There at the window, with the curtains pushed aside, was the enormous long pale wrinkly face of the Giant Person, staring in. The flashing black eyes were fixed on Sophie's bed.

The next moment, a huge hand with pale fingers came snaking in through the window. This was followed by an arm, an arm as thick as a tree-trunk, and the arm,   15
the hand, the fingers were reaching out across the room towards Sophie's bed.

This time Sophie really did scream, but only for a second because very quickly the huge hand clamped down over her blanket and the scream was smothered by the bedclothes.

Sophie, crouching underneath the blanket, felt strong fingers grasping hold of   20
her, and then she was lifted up from her bed, blanket and all, and whisked out of the window.

If you can think of anything more terrifying than that happening to you in the middle of the night, then let's hear about it.

The awful thing was that Sophie knew exactly what was going on although she   25
couldn't see it happening. She knew that a Monster (or Giant) with an enormous long pale wrinkly face and dangerous eyes had plucked her from her bed in the middle of the witching hour and was now carrying her out through the window smothered in a blanket.

What actually happened next was this. When the Giant had got Sophie outside,   30
he arranged the blanket so that he could grasp all the four corners of it at once in one of his huge hands, with Sophie imprisoned inside. In the other hand he seized the suitcase and the long trumpet thing and off he ran.

From *The BFG* by Roald Dahl

Underline the correct answers.

1 At what time of day does the passage take place?

(day-time, night-time, can't tell)

2 How was the Giant Person's nose described?

(as long as a knife, as pointed as a knife, as sharp as a knife)

3 Where did Sophie run to?

(the other side of the room, into her bed, behind the curtain)

    3

Answer these questions.

4–5 Give the meaning of the following words as they are used in the passage.

'devilish' (line 4) _____

'crouched' (line 7) _____

6 Why do you think no sound came out when Sophie wanted to scream (line 11)?

_____

7–8 Write two **adjectives** found in the passage that describe the Giant's face.

_____ (line ____)

_____ (line ____)

9–10 Copy the line from the passage where the author communicates directly with the reader. Why do you think he does this?

_____

_____

_____

11–12 Describe the Giant in your own words, using evidence in the passage.

_____

_____

13–15 Describe the way Sophie is feeling as she is carried in the blanket. Include a line or phrase from the passage to support your answer.

_____

_____

_____

    12

Add the **suffix** to each of these words. Don't forget any spelling changes.

E 2

16 shy + ly _____   **17** spy + ed _____

18 try + ed _____   **19** easy + er _____

20 dry + ing _____   **21** cry + ed _____

6

Copy the passage, adding the missing capital letters.

D 6

22–31 suddenly, out of the tunnel emerged the flying scotsman. hannah and leroy had been waiting for this moment, ever since reading about this train in famous trains of the past. they screamed with excitement as it flew past them on its way to banbury.

_____

_____

_____

_____

_____

10

Write two **compound words** that begin with the word in bold.

D 11

32–33 every _____   _____

34–35 candle _____   _____

36–37 rain _____   _____

38–39 play _____   _____

8

Write each of these **adverbs** in a sentence.

D 6

40 angrily

_____

41 stupidly

_____

42 unexpectedly

_____

3

Complete the table of **nouns** below.

43–54 France   love   team   door   sympathy   leg   Nigel

       camel   justice   bunch   swarm   Hyde Park

Common nouns	Proper nouns	Collective nouns	Abstract nouns

Add *cial* or *tial* to complete the words.

55 offi_____

56 confiden_____

57 essen_____

58 commer_____

59 artifi_____

60 par_____

Add an **adjectival phrase** to complete each sentence.

61 Tola slept peacefully in her _____ bed.

62 The _____ fireworks went high in the sky.

63 Alice clutched her _____ teddy.

64 Monty, the _____ dog, bounded through the long grass.

Add a **prefix** to each of these **words** to make a new word.

65 activate   _____

66 join   _____

67 treat   _____

68 embark   _____

69 continue   _____

70 define   _____

71 compose   _____

72 head   _____

Put a *tick* next to the words spelt correctly and a *cross* next to those spelt incorrectly.

E 2

73 shreik _____   74 rein _____

75 leisure _____   76 releive _____

77 niegh _____   78 receive _____

79 seige _____

7

Underline the two **clauses** in each sentence.

D 2

80–81 Aden ran with all his might when he saw the raging bull.

82–83 Julie combed her hair constantly because she wanted straight hair.

84–85 While Yan was painting a picture, the lights suddenly went off.

6

Write a sentence using brackets to indicate parenthesis.

D 5

86–87 _____

_____

Write a sentence using dashes to indicate parenthesis.

88–89 _____

_____

Write a sentence using commas to indicate parenthesis.

90–91 _____

_____

6

Write down three **onomatopoeic** words that can be used with these.

C 4

92–94 fireworks

_____   _____   _____

95–97 rain

_____   _____   _____

98–100 a farmyard

_____   _____   _____

9

Paper 11

What is a hobbit? I suppose hobbits need some description nowadays since they
have become rare and shy to the Big People, as they call us. They are (or were)
a little people, about half our height, and smaller than the bearded Dwarves.
Hobbits have no beards. There is little or no magic about them, except the ordinary
everyday sort which helps them to disappear quietly and quickly when large stupid   5
folk like you and me come blundering along, making a noise like elephants which
they can hear a mile off. They are inclined to be fat in the stomach; they dress in
bright colours (chiefly green and yellow); wear no shoes because their feet grow
natural leather soles and thick warm brown hair like the stuff on their heads (which
is curly); have long brown fingers, good natured faces and laugh deep fruity laughs   10
especially after dinner which they have twice a day when they can get it.

From *The Hobbit* by J R R Tolkien

Underline the correct answers.

1 What magic can hobbits do?

(make themselves smaller, disappear quickly and quietly, make magic shoes)

2 What creatures do hobbits think make a lot of noise?

(elephants, dwarves, people)

3 What colour is a hobbit's skin?

(white, black, pink, brown)

3

Answer these questions.

4 Why might good hearing be an advantage to hobbits?

_____

5–6 Write two reasons why hobbits don't need to wear shoes.

_____

_____

7 Copy the **phrase** from the text that suggests hobbits might enjoy their food.

_____

_____

8 Describe in the context of the passage what 'good natured faces' (line 9–10)
means.

_____

9-11 Find three examples where the writer highlights the differences between the 'Big People' and hobbits.

_____

_____

_____

12-14 Imagine you are a hobbit. Write a short passage describing what you feel about the 'Big People'. Use information from the text to support your answer.

_____

_____

_____

_____

11

Circle only the words that _are not_ **homophones**.

E 2

15-23 diner   dinner   vain   vein   vane   bath   bathe

cite   site   sight   sit   through   threw   thorough

rain   reign   rein   passed   past   pasted

grisly   grizzly   lung   lunge   missed   mist

9

Change these words into their **singular** form.

E 2

24 skies   _____   25 lives   _____

26 lorries   _____   27 giraffes   _____

28 oxen   _____   29 posies   _____

6

Write three sentences, each sentence must include two **possessive pronouns**.

D 5

Underline each **possessive pronoun**.

30-31 _____

32-33 _____

34-35 _____

6

Add a **conjunction** to complete each sentence.

36 The rain poured in through the window _____ no one noticed.

37 I knew where my toothbrush should be _____ I couldn't find it.

38 The dog scratched at the door _____ someone let him in.

39 I like fish and chips _____ I am feeling hungry.

40 Sheena loves reading _____ also writing stories.

41 Deano was tired _____ he didn't want to go to bed.

6

E 2

Choose the correct **prefix** to complete each word.

bi   circum   auto   tele

42 _____phone

43 _____motive

44 _____navigate

45 _____plane

46 _____vision

47 _____biography

48 _____scope

49 _____focals

8

Complete the table below.

strange	coffee	really	jumped	into	of
curly	with	truly	it	himself	threw
almost	thin	going	you	horror	scoundrel

50–67

Nouns	Verbs	Adjectives	Adverbs	Prepositions	Pronouns

18

Add *was* or *were* in each gap to complete each sentence.

68–69 They _____ ready to go swimming but the pool _____ not open.

70 All the children had finished their lunch and _____ ready to go out to play.

71–72 They _____ queuing for hours as the film _____ supposed to be brilliant.

73 Sam wondered whether it _____ time to get up.

Choose a word to complete each expression.

blanket   fence   head   rat   seat   leaf   horse

74 to hang your _____

75 to be a wet _____

76 to turn over a new _____

77 to take a back _____

78 to put the cart before the _____

79 to smell a _____

80 to sit on the _____

Use each of these **prepositions** in an amusing sentence.

81 against

_____

82 between

_____

83 through

_____

84 below

_____

Complete the table below by matching each word to its country of origin. For example the word café originated from France.

85–92 café   gondola   boutique   macaroni   tortilla

mosquito   opera   armadillo   adieu

France	Spain	Italy
café		

8

D 5

Write a **contraction** for each of these pairs of words.

93 we shall   _____   **94** they will   _____

95 should not   _____   **96** I have   _____

97 has not   _____   **98** will not   _____

99 there is   _____   **100** you are   _____

8

Now go to the Progress Chart to record your score!   Total   100

Paper 12

B

There is an old legend about Delhi (the capital of India). Long ago an old Hindu king
was hammering a large iron nail into the earth, and as he swung with all his might
the tip of the nail struck the head of the snake-god who supports the world on his
coiled body. The king trembled at the thought of the snake-god's anger – would he
bring fire and plague to his subjects, or even destroy the world? He ordered all his   5
subjects to offer prayers and sacrifices to placate the snake-god. Several months
passed and when the god's anger was soothed he told the king that he wouldn't
punish him, but he said that on that spot there would always be war and unrest.
    The iron nail in this fable is supposed to be the Iron Pillar which today stands in the
courtyard of a tower built about six hundred years ago. There is another legend which   10
says that if you stand with your back to the pillar and can stretch your arms behind you
around the pillar, all your wishes will come true. Many people have tried to do this but
no one has had arms long enough to get more than half way round the pillar!

Underline the correct answers.

  1 In which country is the city of Delhi?

    (India, Iran, Indonesia)

  2 What are the king's 'subjects'?

    (words, people, thoughts, towns)

  3 How long ago was the tower that houses the Iron Pillar built?

    (sixty years ago, six thousand years ago, six hundred years ago)

Answer these questions.

  4 In the context of this passage, what does the **phrase** 'with all his might' (line 2)
    mean?

_____

5–6 What evidence is there that the king was concerned for his kingdom? Include a line or **phrase** from the passage to support your answer.

_____

_____

7 Write another word or **phrase** for 'sacrifices' (line 6).

_____

8–9 In your own words describe how you as the Hindu king might have felt the moment the nail struck the head of the snake-god. Explain why you would feel this way.

_____

_____

10–11 If you were the Hindu king and one day all your wishes were granted, what would you wish for?

_____

8

E 2

Add the **prefix** in or im to each of these words.

12 _____perfect   **13** _____correct   **14** _____accurate

15 _____pure   **16** _____balance   **17** _____complete

18 _____patient   **19** _____visible

8

D 12

Rewrite these direct speech sentences into **reported speech**.

20 "Time for dinner," called Mum.

_____

21 "Can we go out to play?" asked the children.

_____

22 "I'm hiding in the shed," David whispered to Amie.

_____

23 "It is really cold today," mumbled the postman.

_____

24 "I love my new shoes," exclaimed Gina.

_____

5

Write an **onomatopoeic** word for each of the following.

C 4

25 a bag of crisps   _____

26 out of breath   _____

27 tramping through mud   _____

28 a bouncing ball   _____

29 closing a door   _____

30 diving in water   _____

31 a watch alarm   _____

7

Add the **suffix** *ed* to each of these words. Make any necessary spelling changes.

E 2

32 fit   _____   33 carry   _____

34 knot   _____   35 pick   _____

36 marry   _____   37 hunt   _____

6

Write each of these pairs of short sentences as one sentence.

D 1

38 Tom ate his food. He was very hungry.

_____

39 The sun shone brightly. It woke Gemma up.

_____

40 The school trip was great fun. They didn't want to go home.

_____

41 Nasar learnt his spelling homework. He still got some wrong in the test.

_____

_____

4

Write whether each of these sentences is in the **past**, **present** or **future tense**.

D 6

42 The dog licked Grant.   _____

43 Caitlin was swimming.   _____

44 Len is sleeping.   _____

45 The chicken is laying an egg.   _____

46 I shall not be home till six o'clock. _____

47 Cleo ate her food. _____

48 Rachel will go to Matthew's house. _____

7

D 6

Write the words in the correct columns of the table.

49–60 stumbled   frantically   because   of   silky   among

heaved   beauty   stupidly   fluffy   bread   although

Noun	Adjective	Verb	Adverb	Preposition	Conjunction

12

D 9

Write a **synonym** for each word in bold.

61 I **attempted** to climb the rock. _____

62 She was **requested** to sit down and wait. _____

63 He **remarked** that he was cold and tired. _____

64 The picture **adhered** to the paper. _____

65 She **frequently** went to see her grandmother. _____

66 Jack was **awarded** the first prize. _____

67 Shaun's family was very **wealthy**. _____

68 At the concert we **applauded** loudly. _____

8

E 2

D 6

Remove the **suffix** of these **abstract nouns** to make a **verb**.

69 attraction _____

70 entertainment _____

71 departure _____

72 attachment _____

73 failure _____

74 completion _____

6

Fill in the missing words in this poem.

A stranger called this morning
Dressed all in black and grey
Put every sound into a bag

75 And carried them ___away___

The whistling of the kettle
The turning of the lock
The purring of the kitten

76 The ticking of the ___clock___

The popping of the toaster
The crunching of the flakes
When you spread the marmalade

77 The scraping noise it ___makes___

The hissing of the frying-pan
The ticking of the grill
The bubbling of the bathtub

78 As it starts to ___fill___

The drumming of the raindrops
On the window-pane
When you do the washing-up

79 The gurgle of the ___drain___

The crying of the baby
The squeaking of the chair
The swishing of the curtain

80 The creaking of the ___stair___

A stranger called this morning
He didn't leave his name
Left us only silence

81 Life will never be the ___same___

'The Sound Collector' by Roger McGough

Rewrite these sentences without double negatives.

82 I haven't got no money.

_____

83 There wasn't no clown at the circus.

_____

84 There weren't no sweets in the jar.

_____

85 Tina hasn't no umbrella for the rain.

_____

4

D 4
D 5

Rewrite the following correctly.

86–100 quick come here called tom
the rain was falling heavily and they wanted to avoid getting wet
when do you think it will stop asked misha

_____

_____

_____

_____

15

Now go to the Progress Chart to record your score!   **Total**   100

Progress Chart   English 9–10 years Book 1

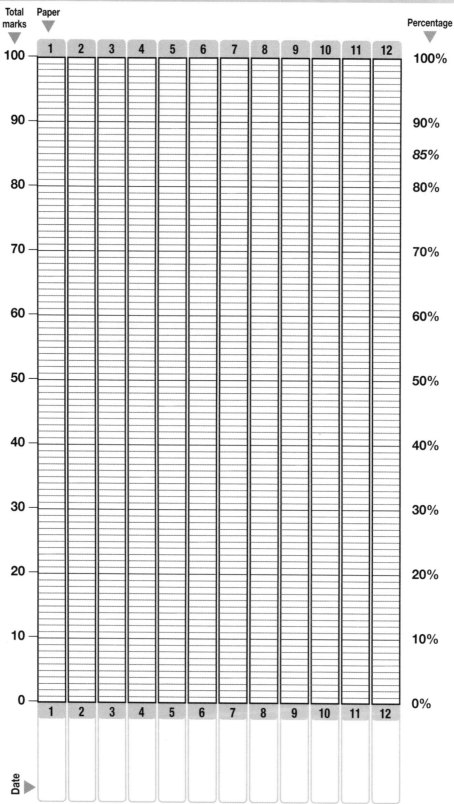

When you've finished the book use the Next Step Planner

WORKBOOK 2.0

FINDING #HAPPILYEVERAFTER IN A #MARRIAGESUCKS WORLD

COUNTER CULTURE

#legalstuff

CounterCulture Marriage
Finding #happilyeverafter in a #marriagesucks world

Workbook, Edition 2.0

Published by Edify Publishing
3446 Winder Highway
Suite M195
Flowery Branch, GA 30542

info@counterculturemin.com
www.counterculturemin.com

Editorial content by Robert & Gloria Stella
Workbook design and layout by Gloria Stella

ISBN: 978-1-7339305-0-5

Printed and bound in the United States of America

10 9 8 7 6 5 4 3 2 1

TABLE OF CONTENTS
#topics

#truth
"The world has grown suspicious of anything that
looks like a happily married life."
@Oscar Wilde

"You're going to find that there will be times when people will have no stomach for solid teaching, but will fill up on spiritual junk food - catchy opinions that tickle their fancy. They'll turn their backs on truth and chase mirages. But you -- keep your eye on what you're doing; accept the hard times along with the good; keep the Message alive; do a thorough job as God's servant."
-2 Timothy 4:3-5 (MSG)

A NOTE FROM ROBERT & GLORIA STELLA

In our culture, we see how marriages operate in the latest blockbusters, the most popular sitcoms and the articles that highlight the woes of the latest celebrity gossip. As we observe these cultural examples, without realizing it, we adopt many of those same philosophies into our own marriages and then wonder why we can't seem to get that "happily ever after" that we believe God intended for us. The truth is, many of us don't achieve the "happy ever after" because we may not be following the method given to us by the One where true "happiness" comes from.

It is our desire that this study reveals some of the ways that today's culture has infiltrated your marriage so you can make an informed decision of how you want to proceed. Hosea 4:6 states, "my people are destroyed for lack of knowledge." Once the knowledge from God's Word has been revealed to you for your marriage, we hope that the topics will generate a flurry of conversations and dialogue between your group and privately with your spouse. We do believe in "happily ever afters". We believe in marriages that can work through any obstacle together and come out on the other side a happier and stronger couple, working closer together towards the purpose that God has on their lives.

GETTING THE MOST OUT OF THIS STUDY

THE WORKBOOK.
Fill-in the answers for each session as you read each corresponding chapter in "CounterCulture Marriage" by Robert & Gloria Stella. The answers to the fill-in-the-blanks are also written in the Leader Notes section in the back of the workbook.

THE DISCUSSION.
After you have read the book, utilize the discussion questions in the workbook to facilitate conversations related to the topic. Use the #culture story at the beginning of each session as an opportunity to discuss and "counsel" the #culture couple as a group. Sample answers and discussion points for the leader to direct their group for each question is located in the Leader Notes section in the back of the workbook.

THE EVALUATIONS.
This is our favorite part of the study and possibly the most important part! The evaluations are intended for you and your spouse to have the opportunity to apply what was taught and discussed directly to your own lives. Each person should evaluate themselves and their spouse WITHOUT sharing your answers until both spouses have completed the evaluation. Afterwards, compare your answers and discuss privately with your spouse. You may be surprised at the difference between how you rated yourself and how your spouse rated you. Use this as a conversation starter. Remember to share your responses and receive your spouse's ratings with LOVE!

THE BUSINESS OF MARRIAGE

#friendship

#culture
"Happiness in marriage is entirely a matter of chance."
@Jane Austen

#CULTURE

Drew and Vanessa have been married for a couple years after dating for several months. While they were dating, their friends would always comment on how great it was that they enjoyed each other's company so much...nothing better than marrying your best friend!

Of course, since getting married and having to deal with life's responsibilities, just "hangin' out" has made it's way to the bottom of the priority list. Now they are expecting their first child and with the couple already barely making ends meet, the stress level in the house has skyrocketed. Every time they are together, there is bound to be a blow-out fight and they simply don't enjoy being around each other anymore.

Out of sheer desperation, Vanessa signs them up for counseling sessions, marriage classes and buys multiple marriage books. Although Drew is cooperative, he's burned out and all Vanessa ever wants to talk about are things they need to change or the latest method to "fix your marriage" she wants to try. She's so busy planning and organizing that they haven't really spent a lot of time enjoying the bedroom (if you know what we mean). Marriage has become an obligation and a very large to-do list for Drew and he has learned to take advantage of every opportunity he gets to get away from it all.

#COUNTERCULTURE

When people refer to the "honeymoon stage", they are referring to the beginning of their marriage, when life is bliss. When we had the time and the desire to focus exclusively on our new spouse and were excited about the adventure of forging a new life together. Then life gets busy and our focus starts to shift to all the things we need to accomplish to survive. Let's challenge the notion of a "honeymoon stage" existing at all. A "stage" insinuates an attitude during a period of time that can rarely be recaptured. What if the "honeymoon stage" is actually the result of a series of choices and by making different choices, you can recapture the "honeymoon stage" permanently in your marriage?

Marriage is not a contract. It's a _____.

1. RE: CONNECT

_____ your spouse - we change several times in our lifetimes, so there will always be something

new to learn about your spouse

_____ with your spouse - your mind is a powerful thing and if you want to, you can find something

that you can become interested in alongside your spouse

_____ your spouse - set apart time on a regular basis to enjoy your spouse's company as friends -

without talking about kids, finances, stresses or complaints

_____ with your spouse - whether your talking about what you would do with a million dollars or

what you would dream to do one day - never stop dreaming and never stop dreaming together

2. FRENEMIES

Learn to _____ - don't be afraid to let laughter enter your life....or your arguments

> "'A cheerful heart is good medicine, but a broken spirit saps a person's strength."
> -Proverbs 17:22 (NLT)

Compare your spouse to no one - focus on what you have and let God work out everything else

Be careful when grading your marriage - sometimes we can be so focused on achieving a goal for a happy

marriage that we end up missing the "_____" part

Balance advice - marriage advice and classes are great, but each individual and marriage is unique. Apply

what is _____, use advice that is _____, and archive what is

_____ at that time

3. REMOVING STRESS

Get a fresh _____ - if your interactions with your spouse seem to be increasingly

negative, take a step back and do or talk about something fun with your spouse so you can "reset"

the tone

_____ God - if your heart is after God's heart, then you don't have to spend so much effort and

stress trying to determine the outcome of your life

> "'Do not worry then, saying, 'What will we eat?' or 'What will we drink?' or 'What will we wear
> for clothing?' For the Gentiles seek all these things; for your Heavenly Father knows that you
> need all these things. But seek first His kingdom and His righteousness, and all these things
> will be added to you. So do not worry about tomorrow; for tomorrow will care for itself. Each
> day has enough trouble of it's own." -Matthew 6:31-34 (NASB)

4. FIND EACH OTHER IN THE _____ - don't let the tough seasons in life pull you apart,

find ways to use the valleys to push you together

#DISCUSSION

Write your opinions for each question below or discuss your answers with your group/spouse.

QUESTION 1

Go back and review the #culture story on page 3. What are the long-term effects of how Drew and Vanessa handled their situation? In light of the information given in this session, discuss how each of them should have reacted differently.

QUESTION 2

Did you have a "honeymoon" stage? If so, how would you describe it? Why do you think couples don't live in their "honeymoon stage" forever?

QUESTION 3

How do stress and life obligations play a role in your ability to be "friends" with your spouse? What are some ways to rekindle that friendship?

QUESTION 4

How does "taking life too seriously" reflect on your relationship with God?

#SELFEVALUATIONS

Score each statement on a scale of 0-5 (0=Disagree; 5=Agree).

Each spouse should complete their evaluation page privately,
then share and discuss their results together afterwards.

HUSBANDS: EVALUATE YOURSELF

☐ I actively take an interest in my spouse's activities and interests (whether it be participating with them or simply listening to them talk).

☐ I take time to reconnect with my spouse on a regular basis without including "business" (finances, work, children, etc) in our conversation.

☐ I enjoy doing things with my spouse and we have fun together.

☐ I trust God will direct and provide for my life as long as I am focused on growing closer in love and obedience to Him and do not try to control the outcome of every situation.

☐ During our toughest seasons together, I draw closer to my spouse rather than withdraw from him/her (we handle life together, rather than as individuals).

☐ I laugh with my spouse on a regular basis.

☐ I do not force "marriage advice" on our marriage or my spouse.

☐ My Total

HUSBANDS: EVALUATE YOUR WIFE

☐ My spouse actively takes an interest in my activities and interests (whether it be participating with me or simply listening to me talk).

☐ My spouse takes time to reconnect with me on a regular basis without including "business" (finances, work, children, etc) in our conversation.

☐ My spouse enjoys doing things with me and we have fun together.

☐ My spouse trusts God will direct and provide for their life as long as they are focused on growing closer in love and obedience to Him and do not try to control the outcome of every situation.

☐ During our toughest seasons together, my spouse draws closer to me rather than withdrawing from me (we handle life together, rather than as individuals).

☐ My spouse laughs with me on a regular basis.

☐ My spouse does not force "marriage advice" on our marriage or me.

☐ My Spouse's Total

WIVES: EVALUATE YOURSELF

☐ I actively take an interest in my spouse's activities and interests (whether it be participating with them or simply listening to them talk).

☐ I take time to reconnect with my spouse on a regular basis without including "business" (finances, work, children, etc) in our conversation.

☐ I enjoy doing things with my spouse and we have fun together.

☐ I trust God will direct and provide for my life as long as I am focused on growing closer in love and obedience to Him and do not try to control the outcome of every situation.

☐ During our toughest seasons together, I draw closer to my spouse rather than withdraw from him/her (we handle life together, rather than as individuals).

☐ I laugh with my spouse on a regular basis.

☐ I do not force "marriage advice" on our marriage or my spouse.

☐ My Total

WIVES: EVALUATE YOUR HUSBAND

☐ My spouse actively takes an interest in my activities and interests (whether it be participating with me or simply listening to me talk).

☐ My spouse takes time to reconnect with me on a regular basis without including "business" (finances, work, children, etc) in our conversation.

☐ My spouse enjoys doing things with me and we have fun together.

☐ My spouse trusts God will direct and provide for their life as long as they are focused on growing closer in love and obedience to Him and do not try to control the outcome of every situation.

☐ During our toughest seasons together, my spouse draws closer to me rather than withdrawing from me (we handle life together, rather than as individuals).

☐ My spouse laughs with me on a regular basis.

☐ My spouse does not force "marriage advice" on our marriage or me.

☐ My Spouse's Total

HOW HEALTHY IS THE FRIENDSHIP IN YOUR MARRIAGE?
(add your total + your spouse's total)

Combined Total: 54-70	Easy, breezy, beautiful…
Combined Total: 36-53	We need to regroup and reconnect
Combined Total: 18-35	Um….let me try to pencil you in…
Combined Total: 0-17	I have a spouse!? Oh, is that who that is…

WHAT WO/MEN WANT

#respect #security

#funnies
"Women don't want to hear what you think.
Women want to hear what they think - in a deeper voice."
@Bill Cosby

#CULTURE

Philip and Nadia have been married for a couple years and things seem to be going well between them. Unfortunately, things between Nadia and Philip's family (mainly his mom and sister) don't seem to be going so good. Philip's family never seemed to approve of Nadia and although Philip obviously felt differently, Philip has decided that the wisest decision is not to choose sides in the midst of all the family drama...which seems reasonable enough.

One afternoon, Nadia comes home in tears after seeing a status update on her sister-in-law's Facebook page attacking Nadia. The update wasn't direct or overtly accusatory, but for anyone familiar with the ongoing family drama, it was obviously directed towards her. She waits for her husband, Philip, to come home so she can have someone to confide in.

Unfortunately, Philip seems to nonchalantly brush off the status update and questions why Nadia would let something so menial upset her...after all, he's still with her, isn't he? Frustrated with his response, Nadia resorts to calling her best friend and spends the rest of the evening venting about Philip and his family while Philip occasionally strolls across the room and rolls his eyes whenever he hears the insulting comments Nadia makes. When the height of the drama subsides for the evening, Philip and Nadia get a good night's sleep and continue on with their lives. No harm, no foul.

#COUNTERCULTURE

What do wo/men want? If that's not the question of a lifetime, we're not sure what is! Although we can speculate in philosophical terms or give superficial answers that would provide temporary happiness, most of us would be surprised to learn how simple the answer can be. By no means are we claiming that there aren't a slew of answers that would be accurate on some level, but we do believe that God created us with a basic need that represents His ultimate plan for creation. By diving deeper into this topic we can narrow it down to one basic need, both different for males and females. If clearly understood, this knowledge can not only clear up communication with your spouse, but bring a deeper sense of fulfillment in your marriage and life.

1. WHAT DO WE REALLY WANT?

Men need to be _____, deeply admired, _____ and honored for what they

are able to accomplish. In other words, men need to feel _____.

Women need to feel _____, confiden that they are _____ and cherished for who they are,

protected from harm (spiritually, emotionally and physically) and free from _____ and

_____.

2. CHRIST AND THE CHURCH

> "'For this reason a man shall leave his father and mother and be joined to his wife, and the two shall become one flesh.' This is a great mystery, but I speak concerning Christ and the church."
> -Ephesians 5:31-32 (NKJV)

Biblically speaking, the husband represents _____ and the wife represents the _____.

3. WHAT WOMEN WANT: SECURITY

Three types of security that women need:

_____ Security - a husband should demonstrate that he _____ God, puts his _____ in

God and is _____ to God

_____ Security - a husband should prove that he is _____ and protect

his wife's _____

_____ Security - a husband should protect his wife from _____ threats.

Providing security requires _____-_____. Christ sacrificed Himself to provide security to

the church - because it was in the best interest of the church, NOT in His best interest.

4. WHAT MEN WANT: RESPECT

Three ways to show respect:

Giving _____ - a wife should _____ on her husband's admirable qualities

Giving _____ - a wife should consistently _____ her husband privately and publicly

Allow him to _____ - a wife should _____ his opinions, working with him on the best decision for

the family and then ultimately allowing him the honor of making the _____ decision

The more _____ a wife gives her husband, the more _____ he will gain and the

more respect he will _____. Respect is _____, not earned.

"However, each one of you also must love his wife as he loves himself,
and the wife must respect her husband."-Ephesians 5:33 (NIV)

5. THE CYCLE

Security and respect are both built on each other - in order for a husband to gain his wife's respect, she must feel secure and in order for a husband to logistically be able to provide security for his wife, she must allow him to lead the relationship. The cycle must begin with someone somewhere. Regardless of whether or not your spouse is providing your basic need, start providing for theirs.

Nothing melts the heart of a man more than the respect and admiration of his wife and nothing makes a woman respect and admire her husband more than to feel secure in his love and protection.

#DISCUSSION

Write your opinions for each question below or discuss your answers with your group/spouse.

QUESTION 1

Go back and review the #culture story on page 11. What are the long-term effects of how Philip and Nadia handled their situation? In light of the information given in this session, discuss how each of them should have reacted differently.

_____
_____
_____
_____
_____

QUESTION 2

What does culture tell us that wo/men what?

_____
_____
_____
_____

QUESTION 3

What are some things that keep wives from providing the respect that their husbands need?

_____
_____
_____
_____

QUESTION 4

What are some things that keep husbands from providing the security that their wives need?

_____
_____
_____
_____
_____

#SELFEVALUATIONS

Score each statement on a scale of 0-5 (0=Disagree; 5=Agree).

Each spouse should complete their evaluation page privately,
then share and discuss their results together afterwards.

HUSBANDS: EVALUATE YOURSELF

☐ I am providing security for my wife even when she does not deserve it, is taking advantage of it, is wrong or is not respecting me.

☐ I am allowing my wife to meet my need to be respected by being a husband deserving of respect.

☐ I provide emotional security for my wife by not lying, being deceptive or giving her any reason to doubt my honesty.

☐ I provide physical security for my wife by defending her when other people (including family) attack her verbally or physically.

☐ I provide spiritual security for my wife by demonstrating to her (whether directly or indirectly) that my desire is to make decisions according to God's will and purpose for our lives.

☐ My spouse feels highly protected.

☐ My Total

HUSBANDS: EVALUATE YOUR WIFE

☐ My wife provides respect to me even when I do not deserve it, am taking advantage of it, am wrong or am not protecting them.

☐ My wife makes it possible for me to meet her need to be protected by allowing me to protect her.

☐ My wife consistently encourages me so that I feel confident and admired by her.

☐ My wife does not say anything negative or complain about me to or in front of other people (including family).

☐ My wife respects me by ultimately respecting my final decisions - even if she may argue and disagree with my opinions initially.

☐ I feel highly respected.

☐ My Spouse's Total

WIVES: EVALUATE YOURSELF

☐ I am providing respect to my husband even when he does not deserve it, is taking advantage of it, is wrong or is not protecting me.

☐ I am making it possible for my husband to meet my need to be protected by allowing him to protect me.

☐ I consistently encourage my husband so that he feels confident and admired by me.

☐ I do not say anything negative or complain about my husband to or in front of other people (including family).

☐ I respect my husband by ultimately respecting his final decisions - even if I may argue and disagree with his opinions initially.

☐ My husband feels highly respected.

☐ My Total

WIVES: EVALUATE YOUR HUSBAND

☐ My husband provides security to me even when I do not deserve it, am taking advantage of it, am wrong or am not respecting them.

☐ My husband allows me to meet his need to be respected by being a husband deserving of respect.

☐ My husband provides emotional security for me by not lying, being deceptive or giving me any reason to doubt his honesty.

☐ My husband provides physical security for me by defending me when other people (inc. family) attack me verbally or physically.

☐ My husband provides spiritual security for me by demonstrating to me (whether directly or indirectly) that his desire is to make decisions according to God's will and purpose for our lives.

☐ I feel highly protected.

☐ My Spouse's Total

HOW HEALTHY IS THE RESPECT & SECURITY IN YOUR MARRIAGE?
(add your total + your spouse's total)

Combined Total: 46-60	You're both well taken care of!
Combined Total: 31-45	You're almost there.
Combined Total: 15-30	Keep on trekking, don't quit!
Combined Total: 0-14	Umm...

DICTATORS

#leadership

#culture
"Do not put such unlimited power into the hands of husbands.
Remember all men would be tyrants if they could."
@Abigail Adams

#CULTURE

Jackson and Yvonne have always operated the same way: Jackson goes to work and brings home a paycheck and Yvonne, in addition to her career, runs the household. This seems to work for them. After all, Jackson would prefer not to have to worry about any actual responsibilities and Yvonne would prefer to handle everything herself. However, after several years of marriage, with no one to lean on, Yvonne's stress-level has sky-rocketed and she has harvested a growing disdain for Jackson's laziness and inability to "man up". And although Jackson enjoyed his carefree lifestyle for awhile, he has begun to feel a little emasculated by Yvonne and has had a growing desire to be respected by his family.

With little knowledge of how to be a leader except for what he has been exposed to in his years of sitting in front of the TV, Jackson decides to take his house back. Almost out of the blue, he refuses to do what Yvonne tells him to do, begins to stand his ground on his decisions, starts talking down to Yvonne and commanding her to "submit - thou sayeth the Lord." Yvonne, being the strong-willed and independent woman that she is, feels challenged, threatened and dismissed by someone who has taken very little concern in the household affairs up until now. She fights back and the house becomes a war-zone.

#COUNTERCULTURE

Our culture has created two opposing paradigms: a world where husbands are lazy and immature and wives are forced to take the leadership role and another world where the husband rules the house with an iron first and the wife is basically hired help. Both schools of thought are direct contradictions to what God has laid out for our marriages. Although it is true that God intends the husband to lead his wife and family, He also requires the husband to love and serve his wife in such a way that he would give up his life for her. This is called servant-leadership. In order for husbands to fulfill their role as the servant-leader, it is vital that we understand what Biblical leadership is and what it is not.

1. THE STRUCTURE OF LEADERSHIP

God is the head of _____, Christ is the head of every _____, and the husband is the head of his _____.

> "But I want you to understand that the head of every man is Christ, the head of a wife is her husband, and the head of Christ is God." -I Corinthians 11:3 (ESV)

2. YOU ARE NOT A _____

Leadership is not a dictatorship. Dictators rule by force. You, the husband, cannot _____ your

wife to _____ to you.

> "The husband provides leadership to his wife the way Christ does to His church, not by domineering but by cherishing." -Ephesians 5:23 (MSG)

3. LEADERSHIP IS _____

Selflessness in marriage would be your willingness, as a leader, to _____ your own well-being and

_____ for your wife and family.

"Husbands, love your wives, just as Christ loved the church and gave himself up for her."
-Ephesians 5:25 (NIV)

4. LEADERSHIP IS NOT _____

Women were created to do everything a man _____ do. A husband's position of leadership does not make

him more important or more valuable than his wife.

5. SERVANT-LEADERSHIP

Lead with _____ and a _____ attitude.

"Husbands, go all out in your love for your wives, exactly as Christ did for the church - a love
marked by giving, not getting. Christ's love makes the church whole. His words evoke her
beauty. Everything He does and says is designed to bring the best out of her, dressing her in
dazzling white silk, radiant with holiness. And that is how husbands ought to love their wives."
-Ephesians 5:24 (MSG)

_____ yourself to God. The more you allow God to transform you into His image, the better husband

and man you will become.

"And He said to him, 'you shall love the Lord your God with all your heart, and with all your
soul, and with all your mind.'" -Matthew 22:37 (NASB)

Bring God's _____ and _____ into the home. Bring God's love into the house and into everyday

conversations with your family.

Don't be afraid to _____. Being a leader doesn't mean taking on responsbilities that you know

you aren't good at.

Raise your wife's _____ _____. When you, as her husband, are able to recognize her skills and

talents and encourage her to pursue her dreams, it builds her up to a level that is unmatched.

6. HOW TO BE MARRIED TO A SERVANT-LEADER

Let him _____ - your husband can't lead if you haven't vacated the position

Build his _____ - lovingly encourage him to take the lead

Be his _____ - provide input and suggestions in tough decisions

Downplay the _____ - if he fails, don't remind him, just build him back up

#DISCUSSION
Write your opinions for each question below or discuss your answers with your group/spouse.

QUESTION 1
Go back and review the #culture story on page 19. What are the long-term effects of how Jackson and Yvonne handled their situation? In light of the information given in this session, discuss how each of them should have reacted differently.

_____

_____

_____

_____

_____

QUESTION 2
Our culture has veered far away from God's standard of a husband who leads, why do you think that is? What is your initial thought when you hear the words "the head of the house"?

_____

_____

_____

_____

QUESTION 3
What are some ways a husband can lead with love and a servant-leader attitude?

_____

_____

_____

_____

QUESTION 4
How does a husband lead when his wife is unwilling to submit?

_____

_____

_____

_____

_____

#SELFEVALUATIONS

Score each statement on a scale of 0-5 (0=Disagree; 5=Agree).

Each spouse should complete their evaluation page privately,
then share and discuss their results together afterwards.

HUSBANDS: EVALUATE YOURSELF

☐ I am willing and desire to take on the leadership role in my family.

☐ I lead with a servant-leader attitude and with love - leading my wife by serving and protecting her, not forcing her to submit and not holding an attitude of being "the master of my domain"

☐ I do not have a lifestyle (habit, addiction, etc) that is in disobedience to God that may be preventing me from leading my family effectively.

☐ I have put God first in my life and have submitted myself to His authority, so that my wife and family can more easily trust in my leadership.

☐ When decisions need to be made, I discuss the options with my wife and highly respect her opinions.

☐ I make decisions that I believe are best for my family and not because of my selfish desires.

☐ I delegate household responsibilities, in agreement with my wife, according to our strengths and weaknesses.

☐ My Total

HUSBANDS: EVALUATE YOUR WIFE

☐ My wife has vacated the position of "leadership" so that I can fill it.

☐ My wife trusts me to lead the family and if there are uncertainties, she trusts God to take care of the family if/when I make a mistake.

☐ My wife regularly encourages me so that I can lead her with confidence.

☐ My wife is always willing to offer suggestions and input when a decision needs to be made (i.e. she does not leave me in the trenches when I need her help).

☐ If my wife follows my lead and I make a mistake, she does not rub it in or remind me about it later.

☐ If I fail, my wife simply loves me and encourages me to get back up and lead again.

☐ My Spouse's Total

WIVES: EVALUATE YOURSELF

☐ I have vacated the position of "leadership" so that my husband can fill it.

☐ I trust my husband to lead the family and if there are uncertainties, I trust God to take care of the family if/when he makes a mistake.

☐ I regularly encourage my husband so that he can lead me and our children with confidence.

☐ I am always willing to offer suggestions and input when a decision needs to be made (i.e. I do not leave my husband in the trenches when he needs my help).

☐ If I follow my husband's lead and he makes a mistake, I do not rub it in or remind him about it later.

☐ If my husband fails, I simply love my husband and encourage him to get back up and lead again.

☐ My Total

WIVES: EVALUATE YOUR HUSBAND

☐ My husband is willing and desires to take on the leadership role in our family.

☐ My husband leads with a servant-leader attitude and with love - leading me by serving and protecting me, not forcing me to submit and not holding an attitude of being "the master of his domain"

☐ My husband does not have a lifestyle (habit, addiction, etc) that is in disobedience to God that may be preventing him from leading our family effectively.

☐ My husband has put God first in his life and has submitted himself to His authority, so that me and our children can more easily trust in his leadership.

☐ When decisions need to be made, my husband discusses the options with me and highly respects my opinions.

☐ My husband makes decisions that he believes are best for our family and not because of his selfish desires.

☐ My husband delegates household responsibilities, in agreement with me, according to our strengths and weaknesses.

☐ My Spouse's Total

HOW HEALTHY IS LEADERSHIP IN YOUR MARRIAGE?
(add your total + your spouse's total)

Combined Total: 50-65   No Dictators Here!
Combined Total: 34-49   Good Balance
Combined Total: 17-33   Slight Role Adjustment Needed
Combined Total: 0-16   Time to Step It Up...or Down...

DOORMATS

#submission

#truth
"Submission is not about authority and it is not obedience;
it is all about relationships of love and respect."
@Wm Paul Young

#CULTURE

Davis is clearly the "man of the house." He lays down the law with his wife, Elizabeth, and their three children. He certainly has the protective nature of a leader down pat and does make "good" decisions as well. He carries the burdens of the world solely on his shoulders. And Elizabeth? She was well-aware of what she got herself into when she agreed to marry Davis. In fact, that's what made her fall in love with him - his protective and take-charge personality. She genuinely loves that he takes care of everything and she's allowed to stay at home with her children and cook and clean, without having to worry about any of the logistics. The stigma of being a homemaker doesn't bother her.

However, after a decade of marriage, Elizabeth is starting to feel a lack of respect from Davis. She likes that he makes the decisions, but she does want to have a say. She also wants Davis to recognize her contribution to the marriage, his business and the world (other than having kids and keeping house for him). For instance, she has many writing and marketing ideas that his business could really benefit from. Beyond being a mom, she dreams of writing children's books one day and she's good at it, but doesn't know how or where to start. She mentions all of these things to Davis and he listens, but doesn't give it much thought or consideration. It becomes evident to Elizabeth that Davis doesn't view her as a comparable and competent partner in his life. Elizabeth, with her passive demeanor, doesn't argue about it. After all, she is content enough with her life.

#COUNTERCULTURE

When a woman hears that ugly word, "submission", something in her immediately gets defensive and wants to rear her head back and tear off the limbs of the perpetrator! Since the onset of the feminist movement, there has been an uproar anytime a man assumes a more "authoritative" role than a woman. And let's admit it, for most women, their control-freak nature doesn't allow much room to be innately "submissive." Then there's the other end of the spectrum, the women who are so submissive that they forget that their husbands actually need their help and support. Thankfully, God has the perfect solution somewhere in-between and if we will give God's way a chance, we may discover how beautiful and POWERFUL being submissive really is. Submission is not the end of your independence, it's the vehicle to your strength!

1. WHAT IS SUBMISSION?

The word "submit" in these verses is the Greek word, _____, which means to _____ under.

> "Wives, be subject (be submissive and adapt yourselves) to your own husbands as [a service] to the Lord." -Ephesians 5:22 (AMP)

2. THE ARGUMENT FOR SUBMISSION

Another Perspective - as a _____ to God, adjust your attitude and _____ your husband for your

husband's _____.

Submission is a _____ - it's not a preference, feeling or suggestion and the requirement is not void

just because the husband may not be fulfilling his role correctly.

3. MISCONCEPTIONS OF SUBMISSION

Submission can't be _____ - wives have to choose to actively submit, it cannot be forced on them

Submission is about trusting _____ - it's not about how capable, competent or deserving your husband is

Submission does not mean hired _____ - you are not a hired servant and you do not disown your voice

Submissive wife does not mean stay-at-_____ wife - staying at home does not make you a submissive

wife and having a career outside the home does not make you an unsubmissive wife

4. HOW TO SUBMIT

"Now the Lord God said, 'It is not good (sufficient, satisfactory) that the man should be alone; I will make him a helper (suitable, adapted, complementary) for him." -Genesis 2:18 (AMP)

Submission plays to your _____ - each individual has their own unique strengths and weaknesses,

submission shines a spotlight on your strengths

Submit with _____ - submission isn't only about your actions, but also about your attitude

Submit in _____ - you don't get to pick and choose the areas of your life you are willing to submit to

God and your husband

5. HOW TO BE MARRIED TO A SUBMISSIVE WIFE

Let _____ lead you - if your wife trusts that God is leading you, she'll be more willing to let you lead her

_____ your wife - do things that make her feel valuable to you and don't do anything that demeans her

Take _____ - be proactive about decisions that need to be made and be willing to admit mistakes

Put her needs _____ your own - even if it means sacrificing what you want for the well-being of the family

Recognize your _____ for your wife - recognize your weaknesses and know that God has provided a helpmate

#DISCUSSION
Write your opinions for each question below or discuss your answers with your group/spouse.

QUESTION 1
Go back and review the #culture story on page 27. What are the long-term effects of how Davis and Elizabeth handled their situation? In light of the information given in this session, discuss how each of them should have reacted differently.

QUESTION 2
Why do you think that our culture sneers at the thought of a wife being "submissive" to her husband? What is your initial thought when you hear the word "submissive"?

QUESTION 3
Why do women struggle with this concept of submission? What does this say about their trust in God?

QUESTION 4
What does a wife do when her husband refuses to lead?

#SELFEVALUATIONS

Score each statement on a scale of 0-5 (0=Disagree; 5=Agree).

Each spouse should complete their evaluation page privately,
then share and discuss their results together afterwards.

HUSBANDS: EVALUATE YOURSELF

☐ I trust God to lead me as I lead my family.

☐ I make my wife feel valuable and do not do anything that takes that value away from her.

☐ I take responsibility for the decisions that need to be made regarding our family.

☐ I often put my needs above my wife's needs.

☐ I recognize my weaknesses and highlight my wife's strengths.

☐ I view my wife as equally as valuable in her worth and contribution to our marriage.

☐ My Total

HUSBANDS: EVALUATE YOUR WIFE

☐ My wife has left the role of "leader" vacant so I am able to fill that position.

☐ My wife is willing to fulfill the role of a submissive wife...even if she does not feel that I deserve or am ready to be the leader.

☐ If/when I make a mistake, my wife does not hold that mistake over my head.

☐ When a decision needs to be made and my wife disagrees with me, after we have discussed our opinions, she allows me to make the final decision and lets me know that I have her full support.

☐ My wife exhibits patience with me through a "gentle" and "quiet" spirit if I am still figuring out how to be a good leader.

☐ My wife does not undermine my authority in our family.

☐ Our children know, by my wife's example of submission, that I am the head of the household.

☐ My Spouse's Total

WIVES: EVALUATE YOURSELF

☐ I have left the role of "leader" vacant so my husband is able to fill that position.

☐ I am willing to fulfill the role of a submissive wife...even if I do not feel my husband deserves or is ready to be the leader.

☐ If/when my husband makes a mistake, I do not hold that mistake over his head.

☐ When a decision needs to be made and I disagree with my husband, after we have discussed our opinions, I allow him to make the final decision and let him know that he has my full support.

☐ I exhibit patience with my husband through a "gentle" and "quiet" spirit if he is still figuring out how to be a good leader.

☐ I do not undermine my husband's authority in our family.

☐ My children know, by my example of submission, that their father is the head of the household.

☐ My Total

WIVES: EVALUATE YOUR HUSBAND

☐ My husband trusts God to lead Him as he leads our family.

☐ My husband makes me feel valuable and does not do anything that takes that value away from me.

☐ My husband takes responsibility for the decisions that need to be made regarding our family.

☐ My husband often puts my needs above his needs.

☐ My husband recognizes his weaknesses and highlights my strengths.

☐ My husband views me as equally valuable in my worth and contribution to the marriage.

☐ My Spouse's Total

HOW HEALTHY IS SUBMISSION IN YOUR MARRIAGE?
(add your total + your spouse's total)

Combined Total: 50-65	Perfect Partners!
Combined Total: 34-49	Good Balance!
Combined Total: 17-33	Slight Role Adjustment Needed
Combined Total: 0-16	Time to Step It Up...or Down...

OUR PERCEPTION OF DECEPTION

#honesty

#truth
"If you tell the truth, it becomes a part of your past.
If you lie, it becomes a part of your future."
@unknown

#CULTURE

After a long day of shopping, Karen finally finds a dress she loves for her upcoming office party. She's squealing with excitement by the time she gets home and can't wait to show her husband, Nathan, how fabulous she's going to look. Sure enough, he loves the dress...or at least he doesn't see anything wrong with it (as is about the only opinions most men seem to have regarding clothing). Unfortunately, when Karen tries the dress on, it's not flattering...accentuating some areas of her body that she probably would rather keep unaccentuated. Not wanting to hurt her feelings...and definitely not wanting to deal with the usual emotional tirade that has been known to come from negative responses in similar situations, Nathan tells her she looks great and they continue to the party.

After mingling for a couple hours, Karen shares her exciting shopping adventure with her best friend, who replied "maybe you should've gone with a different style", referencing her disapproval for Karen's dress choice. At this statement, Karen is crushed. She immediately turns to Nathan and accuses, "but you told me I looked great," and Nathan replies, "you always look great to me" with a guilty shrug. Now, not only is Karen's confidence shaken, but she's embarrassed because she's been floating through the office for the last two hours mingling with all her co-workers thinking she looked "great." Most of all, she's hurt because she trusted Nathan to be honest with her and because he didn't want to "hurt her feelings", he let her go out in public and embarrass herself. She knew she should've asked her best friend in the first place, at least she knows she can trust her. Fortunately, no MAJOR trust issues developed between Karen and Nathan, because - after all - it's only about a dress. Right?

#COUNTERCULTURE

We are all familiar with the saying "honesty is the best policy" - yet it's a widely accepted practice in our culture to justify dishonesty if it prevents someone's feelings from being hurt. The problem is, the truth always reveals itself and by then, the deceived person is usually postured to endure far greater "hurt feelings" than if they would have been told the truth to begin with. On top of that, our culture also wrongfully associates honesty with rudeness. But the Bible is filled with a balance of scripture that extols truth, while also emphasizing communicating with love and grace. Being able to implement a culture of truth and love within our marriage will ultimately bring us closer to our spouse and cultivate confidence in how we communicate with them.

1. THE WAYS WE DECEIVE

Two things keep people from being completely honest in their marriage: _____ to get what they

want and/or _____ that their opinions and desires will not be well-received.

Four Types of Deception:

_____ - telling your spouse something that you know is not true

_____ - allowing your spouse to believe something inaccurately by withholding information

_____ - telling your spouse something that may be true but for ulterior motives

_____ - exercising your influence to get the results that you desire

2. DECEPTION HURTS

Deception breaches marital _____ - your spouse should never have to decide whether or not you are

being completely honest

3. MOVING TOWARDS HONESTY

Deception puts a _____ in the foundation for your marriage - while deception may appear to

provide a temporary fix, you damage your marriage in the long-run

Eliminate Deception:

Be honest with _____ and God - the first step to not deceiving your spouse, is by not

deceiving yourself

Be an _____ _____ - the quickest route between two points is a straight line; every unknown

piece of information is a loophole and every flatter and manipulation is a detour

"For there is nothing covered that will not be revealed, not hidden that will not be known."
-Luke 12:2 (NKJV)

Communicate with _____ and _____ - how you give and receive truth either reinforces or

punishes your spouse for their decision to be honest with you

"A fool has no delight in understanding, but in expressing his own heart."
-Proverbs 18:2 (NKJV)

Learn some _____ and _____ - be careful not to use your power within the marriage

to get what only you want and what only you want now

Form a relationship of _____ - view your spouse as your helpmate, not your probation officer

"Faithful are the wounds of a friend, but the kisses of an enemy are deceitful."
-Proverbs 27:6 (NKJV)

Use _____ - there is balance between being totally honest and brutally negative - find it

#DISCUSSION

Write your opinions for each question below or discuss your answers with your group/spouse.

QUESTION 1

Go back and review the #culture story on page 35. What are the long-term effects of how Nathan and Karen handled their situation? In light of the information given in this session, discuss how each of them should have reacted differently.

_____

_____

_____

_____

_____

QUESTION 2

Follow the path of deception in a marriage. What is the ultimate outcome? If ultimately, the marriage is hurt, then what keeps us from being open and honest with our spouses?

_____

_____

_____

_____

QUESTION 3

What are the benefits to being totally honest and direct, even if it means an occasional disagreement?

_____

_____

_____

_____

QUESTION 4

What are some examples of keeping the balance between being totally honest and being brutally negative and harmful to the marriage?

_____

_____

_____

_____

_____

#SELFEVALUATIONS

Score each statement on a scale of 0-5 (0=Disagree; 5=Agree).

Each spouse should complete their evaluation page privately,
then share and discuss their results together afterwards.

HUSBANDS: EVALUATE YOURSELF

☐ I do not give my spouse exaggerated/false compliments or bribes in order to get what I want and when I do give my spouse a compliment or do something nice for them (gift, chores, etc), I do so out of love and not because I expect something in return.

☐ I do not manipulate/bribe my spouse by making them feel bad (i.e. guilt trip) or by withholding resources (i.e. sex/money) in order to get my way.

☐ I do not have any secret accounts, passwords, feelings and/or other information that my spouse does not know about.

☐ I am able to share my true feelings, opinions and/or other information with my spouse, and if it may be hurtful to them, I share the information in a loving and gracious manner.

☐ If my spouse shares their true feelings, opinions and/or other information with me that I find hurtful or I do not understand, I am still able to receive it in love and I do not overreact, become defensive or try to retaliate hurtfully.

☐ I am able to confide in my spouse as an accountability partner because they help me with my issues as my helpmate.

☐ I do not use "total honesty" as justification to be brutally negative, degrade or belittle my spouse.

☐ My Total

HUSBANDS: EVALUATE YOUR WIFE

☐ My spouse does not give me exaggerated/false compliments or bribes in order to get what they want and when they do give me a compliment or do something nice for me (gift, chores, etc), they do so out of love and not because they expect something in return.

☐ My spouse does not manipulate/bribe me by making me feel bad (i.e. guilt trip) or by withholding resources (i.e. sex/money) in order to get their way.

☐ My spouse does not have any secret accounts, passwords, feelings and/or other information that I do not know about.

☐ My spouse is able to share their true feelings, opinions and/or other information with me, and if it may be hurtful to me, they share the information in a loving and gracious manner.

☐ If I share my true feelings, opinions and/or other information with my spouse that they find hurtful or they do not understand, they are still able to receive it in love and they do not overreact, become defensive or try to retaliate hurtfully.

☐ My spouse is able to confide in me as an accountability partner because I help them with their issues as their helpmate.

☐ My spouse does not use "total honesty" as justification to be brutally negative, degrade or belittle me.

☐ My Spouse's Total

WIVES: EVALUATE YOURSELF

- [ ] I do not give my spouse exaggerated/false compliments or bribes in order to get what I want and when I do give my spouse a compliment or do something nice for them (gift, chores, etc), I do so out of love and not because I expect something in return.

- [ ] I do not manipulate/bribe my spouse by making them feel bad (i.e. guilt trip) or by withholding resources (i.e. sex/money) in order to get my way.

- [ ] I do not have any secret accounts, passwords, feelings and/or other information that my spouse does not know about.

- [ ] I am able to share my true feelings, opinions and/or other information with my spouse, and if it may be hurtful to them, I share the information in a loving and gracious manner.

- [ ] If my spouse shares their true feelings, opinions and/or other information with me that I find hurtful or I do not understand, I am still able to receive it in love and I do not overreact, become defensive or try to retaliate hurtfully.

- [ ] I am able to confide in my spouse as an accountability partner because they help me with my issues as my helpmate.

- [ ] I do not use "total honesty" as justification to be brutally negative, degrade or belittle my spouse.

- [ ] My Total

WIVES: EVALUATE YOUR HUSBAND

- [ ] My spouse does not give me exaggerated/false compliments or bribes in order to get what they want and when they do give me a compliment or do something nice for me (gift, chores, etc), they do so out of love and not because they expect something in return.

- [ ] My spouse does not manipulate/bribe me by making me feel bad (i.e. guilt trip) or by withholding resources (i.e. sex/money) in order to get their way.

- [ ] My spouse does not have any secret accounts, passwords, feelings and/or other information that I do not know about.

- [ ] My spouse is able to share their true feelings, opinions and/or other information with me, and if it may be hurtful to me, they share the information in a loving and gracious manner.

- [ ] If I share my true feelings, opinions and/or other information with my spouse that they find hurtful or they do not understand, they are still able to receive it in love and they do not overreact, become defensive or try to retaliate hurtfully.

- [ ] My spouse is able to confide in me as an accountability partner because I help them with their issues as their helpmate.

- [ ] My spouse does not use "total honesty" as justification to be brutally negative, degrade or belittle me.

- [ ] My Spouse's Total

HOW HEALTHY IS THE HONESTY IN YOUR MARRIAGE?
(add your total + your spouse's total)

Combined Total: 54-70   It's all flowers and sunshine!
Combined Total: 36-53   Are you hiding something?
Combined Total: 18-35   Back to the drawing board.
Combined Total: 0-17   Stop the presses. Let's talk.

FIGHTING FAIRLY

#arguing

#CULTURE

Jake and Bella have been married for a few years and are best friends. They do everything together and have a great marital friendship - except for this one little thing about Jake that has really started eating away at Bella. In the few occasions when they disagree about something, Jake shuts down completely - he won't express his thoughts, discuss anything or make a decision. This didn't used to bother Bella. She simply took it as an opportunity to do whatever she wanted. But lately, she's been wanting more of a partner in life than just someone to hang out with.

Today, Bella has had enough. She's brought up different topics of disagreement nearly everyday for the last week and Jake refuses to engage in the conversation. She forced another conversation this morning, causing Jake to retreat to his phone. Bella flips-out and begins her self-escalating rant ranging on everything from his haircut to dissatisfaction with their car and finally ending on her dissatisfaction with their marriage. She storms out of the house to take a drive and leaves Jake with his thoughts. Jake turns back to his phone and thinks to himself, "she's obviously PMSing - she'll calm down, come back, get some sleep and be her usual happy go-lucky self in the morning." Jake is right. Bella comes back and gets some rest and shelves the issue - for now.

#COUNTERCULTURE

In our culture, people tend to view arguing as a negative trait in a marriage - so much so that they have convinced themselves that not communicating at all is a better outcome than arguing. We beg to differ. How can you possibly operate as "one flesh" if you don't communicate about the majority of who you are or how you really feel for fear of an argument? If there is no acknowledgment of a problem or difference in opinion, there can be no resolution. Leo Tolstoy once said "what counts in making a happy marriage is not so much how compatible you are, but how you deal with incompatibility."

1. ARGUING IS NOT A BAD THING

Defining the terms disagree, argue and fight according to the Merriam-Webster dictionary:

Disagree - to have a _____ opinion or to fail to agree

Argue - to cause (someone) to _____ to do or not do something by giving _____

Fight - to be involved in (a _____, struggle, etc.) or to argue in an _____ way

Arguing is beneficial to a marriage as it provides a platform to discuss the reasons why you disagree. The issue then, is that we learn HOW to argue so that it doesn't turn into a fight.

2. CONSENT TO COMMUNICATE

Consent to Communicate is when both spouses agree to be _____ to speak about anything in your

life truthfully and not withholding anything.

3. COMMUNICATE CALMLY

Calm Communication is not _____ or _____ harshly or rashly in an argument.

> *"But, speaking the truth in love, may grow up in all things into Him who is the head - Christ -"*
> *-Ephesians 4:15 (NKJV)*

E.S.E.F.

_____ - communicate that you understand how your spouse feels "oh yea, that's tough" "I understand"

_____ - let them know that you are there to help "is there anything I can do?" or give them a hug

_____ - build them back up "we'll get through this" "God has a plan" "it'll be ok"

_____ - if still needed, work together to find a solution

4. COMMUNICATE CONCISELY

Concise Communication is being able to stay on the _____ of an argument or discussion and

_____ the issue.

5. THE AFTERMATH: Resolutions

When a decision must be made - after all is said and done, husbands should make the decision that is best for

the _____-_____ of his wife and children and wives should _____ their

husband's decision and _____ to it with a _____ attitude

When there are deep-seated issues - not all resolutions come overnight; get _____,

_____ it if/when the time is right, but don't _____ it

When your spouse isn't perfect - just as God extended us _____, we must learn to do the same

When it's a one-sided effort - give them _____ to ponder what you've said, _____ for them and

continue to _____ them

When your spouse confesses something - _____ and _____; in most cases, your spouse

is just as trapped by a sin as you are hurt by it

If we are married, then we are married to someone who is failing in some way. We can respond to those failures and become bitter and resentful people or we can respond to those failures in a way that draws us closer to our spouse and God.

#DISCUSSION
Write your opinions for each question below or discuss your answers with your group/spouse.

QUESTION 1
Go back and review the #culture story on page 43. What are the long-term effects of how Jake and Bella handled their situation? In light of the information given in this session, discuss how each of them should have reacted differently.

QUESTION 2
Culturally, people tend to think that a "best friend" is someone we can tell anything to, but many people do not feel comfortable communicating with their spouses on the same level, why do you think that is?

QUESTION 3
Every couple has a different chemistry, what are some ways that you have found works for you in being able to communicate openly, calmly and concisely when things get heated?

QUESTION 4
When we think of how God reacts to us when we disappoint Him, how does that indicate how we should react with our spouse when they disappoint us?

#SELFEVALUATIONS

Score each statement on a scale of 0-5 (0=Disagree; 5=Agree).

Each spouse should complete their evaluation page privately,
then share and discuss their results together afterwards.

HUSBANDS: EVALUATE YOURSELF

[ ] I understand that my spouse (like myself) is not perfect and I do not get easily upset every time they do something that I do not like.

[ ] When my spouse confronts me about something that may make me upset, I remain calm and genuinely try to understand what they are trying to say.

[ ] If I share something with my spouse that may be hurtful, I tell them in a loving way and make sure they believe that they are still accepted and loved by me.

[ ] If we are in a heated discussion/argument, I do not bring up other issues or start name calling.

[ ] Even if I have to take a break to calm down, I feel that I am able to return to a discussion until a resolution or understanding is met instead of avoiding or burying an issue.

[ ] Excluding counseling or mentor relationships, I do not rant to other individuals or on social media regarding issues I am having with my spouse.

[ ] When my spouse is upset or disagrees with me, I try to empathize and support her first, before attempting to fix the situation or defend myself.

[ ] My Total

HUSBANDS: EVALUATE YOUR WIFE

[ ] My spouse understands that I am not perfect and they do not get easily upset every time I do something that they do not like.

[ ] When I confront my spouse about something that may make them upset, they remain calm and genuinely try to understand what I am trying to say.

[ ] If my spouse shares something with me that may be hurtful, they tell me in a loving way and make sure I believe that I am still accepted and loved by them.

[ ] If we are in a heated discussion/argument, my spouse does not bring up other issues or start name calling.

[ ] Even if my spouse has to take a break to calm down, I feel that they are able to return to a discussion until a resolution or understanding is met instead of avoiding or burying an issue.

[ ] Excluding counseling or mentor relationships, my spouse does not rant to other individuals or on social media regarding issues they are having with me.

[ ] When I am upset or disagree with my spouse, she tries to empathize and support me first, before attempting to fix the situation or defend herself.

[ ] My Spouse's Total

WIVES: EVALUATE YOURSELF

☐ I understand that my spouse (like myself) is not perfect and I do not get easily upset every time they do something that I do not like.

☐ When my spouse confronts me about something that may make me upset, I remain calm and genuinely try to understand what they are trying to say.

☐ If I share something with my spouse that may be hurtful, I tell them in a loving way and make sure they believe that they are still accepted and loved by me.

☐ If we are in a heated discussion/argument, I do not bring up other issues or start name calling.

☐ Even if I have to take a break to calm down, I feel that I am able to return to a discussion until a resolution or understanding is met instead of avoiding or burying an issue.

☐ Excluding counseling or mentor relationships, I do not rant to other individuals or on social media regarding issues I am having with my spouse.

☐ When my spouse is upset or disagrees with me, I try to empathize and support him first, before attempting to fix the situation or defend myself.

☐ My Total

WIVES: EVALUATE YOUR HUSBAND

☐ My spouse understands that I am not perfect and they do not get easily upset every time I do something that they do not like.

☐ When I confront my spouse about something that may make them upset, they remain calm and genuinely try to understand what I am trying to say.

☐ If my spouse shares something with me that may be hurtful, they tell me in a loving way and make sure I believe that I am still accepted and loved by them.

☐ If we are in a heated discussion/argument, my spouse does not bring up other issues or start name calling.

☐ Even if my spouse has to take a break to calm down, I feel that they are able to return to a discussion until a resolution or understanding is met instead of avoiding or burying an issue.

☐ Excluding counseling or mentor relationships, my spouse does not rant to other individuals or on social media regarding issues they are having with me.

☐ When I am upset or disagree with my spouse, he tries to empathize and support me first, before attempting to fix the situation or defend himself.

☐ My Spouse's Total

HOW HEALTHY IS THE COMMUNICATION IN YOUR MARRIAGE?
(add your total + your spouse's total)

Combined Total: 54-70	Tie!
Combined Total: 36-53	Fair Fight.
Combined Total: 18-35	Round 3.
Combined Total: 0-17	Knockout.

MORE MONEY, MY MONEY, NO MONEY

#money

#culture
"A woman's best protection is a little money of her own."
@Clare Boothe Luce

#CULTURE

Perry and Susan have been married nearly five years. They have three children - two of which came from Susan's previous marriage. They both have great paying jobs and although they can't spend without limitations, they live very comfortably. Despite the abundance of financial resources flowing into the house, money still finds a way to be the topic of many hot debates in the house.

Because Perry "makes more money", he always feels entitled to buy whatever he wants, leaving Susan to figure the finances out on her own. Fortunately, they come up with a great idea: they decide to each open their own accounts and split all the expenses of life 50/50. This works great for a few months, but Perry starts getting bitter about all the expenses coming from the kids' extra-curricular expenses. Reluctantly, Susan agrees that since two of the children were exclusively hers and she receives the child support into her account, that she should pay for their extra-curricular activities. This type of divisive decision-making continues for a few more months as they both try to figure out how to "fairly" handle their expenses.

Unfortunately, Perry's company goes south and he loses his job and is unable to pay his portion of the bills. At this point, Susan has become a little fed up with Perry's insanely tedious nit-picking over dividing household expenses. She figures she'll let Perry fret for a few weeks. Thankfully, she's not as avid of a spender as Perry and has been saving up for quite a few years for a "rainy day" in an unknown account, so she feels confident she can take care of the family on her own. She agrees to pick up all the household expenses while Perry unsuccessfully looks for a new job. This financial shift makes Susan the "head of the household" and Perry is powerless to say otherwise; after all, he set up the system. After awhile, Perry's constant depressive state starts to takes it's toll on Susan. The burden of caring for the entire family and making all the decisions starts to cause Susan to question Perry's worth to the family. She decides to give it a few more months and see how things go.

#COUNTERCULTURE

Money is one of the most argued about topics in marriage today. Statistics have shown that nearly 45 percent of divorces result from disputes over money. However, if we dig a little deeper, it's not difficult to see that the issue really isn't about money at all, but how we approach life and our marriage.

1. MORE MONEY

Be content - don't _____ your current standard of living with your parents or your friends

> "Then I observed that most people are motivated to success because they envy their neighbors.
> But this, too, is meaningless - like chasing the wind." -Ecclesiastes 4:4 (NLT)

Change your _____ - we are not called to live according to the world's standard, but to God's standard

> "The seed cast in the weeds represents the ones who hear the kingdom news but are
> overwhelmed with worries about all the things they have to do and all the things they want to
> get. The stress strangles what they heard, and nothing comes of it." -Mark 4:19 (MSG)

Be dependent on _____ - don't use spending as a way to cope with your emotional needs

2. MY MONEY

You and your spouse are _____ flesh - money is not so important that it is above this fact

Whether your money is in joint or separate accounts is not as important as both of you being aware of and managing all financial accounts together.

Keep it _____ - "your money, my money, your bills, my bills" eventually leads to a pattern of thinking

that says "your friends, my friends, your job, my job, your life, my life"

Commit to _____ - if you have no "back-up plan" to leave your marriage, then you are forced,

by the lack of options, to find a way to work it out - prepare for a great marriage, not for an easy divorce.

"So then, they are no longer two but one flesh. Therefore what God has joined together,
let not man separate." -Matthew 19:6 (NKJV)

Accept your _____ - there should be no power struggle in a Biblical marriage, husbands should love his

wife so much that he sacrificially makes decisions in her best-interest; and wives, regardless if her

husband is doing his part, should respect her husband's decisions

"Wives, submit yourselves to your own husbands as you do to the Lord."
-Ephesians 5:22 (NKJV)

No _____ - having separate accounts makes it too easy to hide expenses and activities from your spouse

Learn to work _____ - life is full of conflicts, the goal in your marriage is not to learn how to avoid

all conflict, it's to learn how to work together as a team to solve conflict

3. NO MONEY

Tithe - without tithing, there is no _____ of God's provision

Trust - every financial crisis you go through is an opportunity for _____

Encourage each other- especially in a time of crisis, don't place _____ but continually encourage

each other

Share your thoughts - don't _____ how you feel, allow your spouse the opportunity to _____ you

Remember - every season _____

#DISCUSSION

Write your opinions for each question below or discuss your answers with your group/spouse.

QUESTION 1

Go back and review the #culture story on page 51. What are the long-term effects of how Perry and Susan handled their situation? In light of the information given in this session, discuss how each of them should have reacted differently.

_____

_____

_____

_____

_____

QUESTION 2

Who handles the finances logistically in your marriage? Who makes the final decision regarding your finances? Is there a difference?

_____

_____

_____

_____

QUESTION 3

Who tends to spend all the money? Who tends to be stingy? Discuss how you find balance in being able to buy what you want vs. being good stewards?

_____

_____

_____

_____

QUESTION 4

Are there any good reasons to keep money or a purchase hidden from your spouse? What are some reasons (justified or not) that people hide money. Discuss these.

_____

_____

_____

_____

_____

#SELFEVALUATIONS

Score each statement on a scale of 0-5 (0=Disagree; 5=Agree).

Each spouse should complete their evaluation page privately,
then share and discuss their results together afterwards.

HUSBANDS: EVALUATE YOURSELF

[ ] Material possessions are not a high priority in my life, I do not try to "keep up with the Joneses" and I am not discontent or complain about having to live within our means.

[ ] I have self-control not to spend beyond our means and I do not rely on spending to deal with life stresses (constant vacationing, shopping, hobbies, etc)

[ ] I openly handle my/our finances with my spouse and we work together on a regular basis to make decisions about our budget.

[ ] I am comfortable in my marital role (submission/leadership) in regards to our finances.

[ ] I do not have any past or current separate accounts, stashes or financial habits that my spouse is not aware of.

[ ] I tithe and am able to depend fully on God for financial provision (food/shelter) even in the toughest financial crisis.

[ ] During financial hardship, I encourage my spouse regularly and do not place blame bitterly on my spouse.

[ ] My Total

HUSBANDS: EVALUATE YOUR WIFE

[ ] Material possessions are not a high priority in my spouse's life, they do not try to "keep up with the Joneses" and they are not discontent or complain about having to live within our means.

[ ] My spouse has self-control not to spend beyond our means and they do not rely on spending to deal with life stresses (constant vacationing, shopping, hobbies, etc)

[ ] My spouse openly handles my/our finances with me and we work together on a regular basis to make decisions about our budget.

[ ] My spouse is comfortable in their marital role (submission/leadership) in regards to our finances.

[ ] I do not have any suspicion that my spouse has any past or current separate accounts, stashes or financial habits that I am not aware of.

[ ] My spouse tithes and is able to depend fully on God for financial provision (food/shelter) even in the toughest financial crisis.

[ ] During financial hardship, my spouse encourages me regularly and does not place blame bitterly on me.

[ ] My Spouse's Total

WIVES: EVALUATE YOURSELF

☐ Material possessions are not a high priority in my life, I do not try to "keep up with the Joneses" and I am not discontent or complain about having to live within our means.

☐ I have self-control not to spend beyond our means and I do not rely on spending to deal with life stresses (constant vacationing, shopping, hobbies, etc)

☐ I openly handle my/our finances with my spouse and we work together on a regular basis to make decisions about our budget.

☐ I am comfortable in my marital role (submission/leadership) in regards to our finances.

☐ I do not have any past or current separate accounts, stashes or financial habits that my spouse is not aware of.

☐ I tithe and am able to depend fully on God for financial provision (food/shelter) even in the toughest financial crisis.

☐ During financial hardship, I encourage my spouse regularly and do not place blame bitterly on my spouse.

☐ My Total

WIVES: EVALUATE YOUR HUSBAND

☐ Material possessions are not a high priority in my spouse's life, they do not try to "keep up with the Joneses" and they are not discontent or complain about having to live within our means.

☐ My spouse has self-control not to spend beyond our means and they do not rely on spending to deal with life stresses (constant vacationing, shopping, hobbies, etc)

☐ My spouse openly handles my/our finances with me and we work together on a regular basis to make decisions about our budget.

☐ My spouse is comfortable in their marital role (submission/leadership) in regards to our finances.

☐ I do not have any suspicion that my spouse has any past or current separate accounts, stashes or financial habits that I am not aware of.

☐ My spouse tithes and is able to depend fully on God for financial provision (food/shelter) even in the toughest financial crisis.

☐ During financial hardship, my spouse encourages me regularly and does not place blame bitterly on me.

☐ My Spouse's Total

HOW HEALTHY IS MONEY HANDLED IN YOUR MARRIAGE?
(add your total + your spouse's total)

Combined Total: 54-70   One lucky penny!
Combined Total: 36-53   Heads or tails?
Combined Total: 18-35   Money, Money, Money!
Combined Total: 0-17   The love of money is the root of all evil...

PROVING PRIORITIES PRACTICALLY

#priorities

#culture
"I have my hands full with my kids
and so romance is not high on my list of priorities."
@Pamela Anderson

#CULTURE

Ryan and Stephanie have been married for nearly fifteen years and have had a beautiful marriage. They have a wonderful family with their two children, ages ten and thirteen. Ryan has a great paying job that has allowed Stephanie to stay home to raise their children...which lately has consisted mostly of serving as their personal taxi driver. Stephanie has always dreamed of opening up her own bakery and she and Ryan have decided that this is a good time to start that adventure.

Although Ryan was supportive at first, it seems that the bakery has required much more of Stephanie's time and attention than he realized. Nevertheless, he is happy to support her dreams and has begun to help her out around the house. But Stephanie's frantic obsession with things being done "just right" is driving Ryan and the kids crazy! Of course, Stephanie is much too busy to notice Ryan's increasing aggravation with her constant nitpicking.

Ryan remains patient. He and Stephanie both anticipated that the startup of the bakery would require a lot of energy. However, a couple years later, the bakery is up and running and Stephanie is not showing any signs of slowing down. Technically, the bakery could run on it's own without her there every waking hour, but she feels the need to make sure that every detail is exactly the way it should be - after all, it is her attention to detail that has made the bakery successful in the first place. Ryan begins to feel that his support for Stephanie to start the bakery may not have been the best decision for the family as she clearly doesn't understand the importance for work/life balance.

#COUNTERCULTURE

When something or someone is a priority in your life, you create time to devote to it without excuse. We may claim that our spouse is our priority until we are blue in the face, but if our behaviors do not indiciate that they are a priority or if they do not feel like they are a priority, then they aren't really a priority. First things first: lets establish what our priorities should be. Then let's take a look at some very practical ways to demonstrate those priorities.

The priorities that you demonstrate will define you: who you live for, who you are and what you do.

1. ORDER OF PRIORITIES

#1 First Things First: God - your _____ relationship with God should not only be your top priority, but

an ____-_____ priority that takes precedence in all other priorities

> "Jesus replied: 'Love the Lord your God with all your heart and with all your soul and with all your mind. This is the first and greatest commandment. And the second is like it: Love your neighbor as yourself. All the Law and the Prophets hang on these two commandments.'"
> -Matthew 22:37-40 (NIV)

#2 Love Thy Neighbor: _____ - your spouse is the closest "neighbor" you have and great time should be

devoted to loving and caring for them

#3 All my Children: Children - through demonstrating that _____ and your _____ are your priorities;

there is nothing greater you can give your children than a great example of how a life should be lived

#SELFEVALUATIONS

Rank each group below from 1-5, 1 being the most important to you personally and 5 being the least important.

Each spouse should complete their evaluation page privately, then share the results with eachother afterwards.

GROUP 1 (rank from 1-5):

_____ Encouraging Words (little notes, sweet texts)

_____ Support of Career Aspirations

_____ General Convo (unrelated to business/feelings)

_____ Getting Healthy Together (diet, exercise, etc)

_____ Help with Daily Tasks (without being asked)

GROUP 2 (rank from 1-5):

_____ Sharing Feelings/Emotions with Each Other

_____ Acceptance of Family

_____ Fun/Humor

_____ Small gifts (not given on special occasions)

_____ Sexual Activity

GROUP 3 (rank from 1-5):

_____ Standard of Living (nice house, nice car, etc)

_____ Dates (outside of the house, alone)

_____ Respecting My Opinions

_____ Romance/Passion

_____ Home Cooked Meals

GROUP 4 (rank from 1-5):

_____ Being Understood (spouse not getting frustrated)

_____ Serving/Giving Together (outreach outings, etc)

_____ Recognition/Appreciation (verbally expressed)

_____ Acceptance of Friends

_____ Relaxing and Doing Nothing (tv, sleep, etc)

GROUP 5 (rank from 1-5):

_____ Dressed-Up Spouse

_____ Financial Freedom (debt-free)

_____ Family Time (dinner table, board games)

_____ Well-Kept House

_____ Physical Touch (hugs, holding hands, etc)

Share your rankings with your spouse. What are some ways that you can practically demonstrate to your spouse that they are a priority based on their rankings?

_____

_____

_____

_____

Rank each group below from 1-5, 1 being the most important to you personally and 5 being the least important.

Each spouse should complete their evaluation page privately, then share the results with eachother afterwards.

GROUP 1 (rank from 1-5):

_____ Encouraging Words (little notes, sweet texts)

_____ Support of Career Aspirations

_____ General Convo (unrelated to business/feelings)

_____ Getting Healthy Together (diet, exercise, etc)

_____ Help with Daily Tasks (without being asked)

GROUP 2 (rank from 1-5):

_____ Sharing Feelings/Emotions with Each Other

_____ Acceptance of Family

_____ Fun/Humor

_____ Small gifts (not given on special occasions)

_____ Sexual Activity

GROUP 3 (rank from 1-5):

_____ Standard of Living (nice house, nice car, etc)

_____ Dates (outside of the house, alone)

_____ Respecting My Opinions

_____ Romance/Passion

_____ Home Cooked Meals

GROUP 4 (rank from 1-5):

_____ Being Understood (spouse not getting frustrated)

_____ Serving/Giving Together (outreach outings, etc)

_____ Recognition/Appreciation (verbally expressed)

_____ Acceptance of Friends

_____ Relaxing and Doing Nothing (tv, sleep, etc)

GROUP 5 (rank from 1-5):

_____ Dressed-Up Spouse

_____ Financial Freedom (debt-free)

_____ Family Time (dinner table, board games)

_____ Well-Kept House

_____ Physical Touch (hugs, holding hands, etc)

Share your rankings with your spouse. What are some ways that you can practically demonstrate to your spouse that they are a priority based on their rankings?

_____

_____

_____

_____

EXPECT LESS, APPRECIATE MORE

#expectations #appreciation

#culture
"Whoever you end up with, you shouldn't be changing a thing for them. Nothing.
Don't be with anyone if you can't be you. Because you're bang on just as you are."
@Lucy Robinson

#CULTURE

Eric and Jaclyn just got married a few months ago and things aren't going so well. Since they lived together before they got married, they both figured the transition to married life would be seamless. If anything, Jaclyn expected the transition to "husband" would instill some more maturity in Eric. But alas, he still spends several hours a day playing video games and hanging with the guys with little effort into contributing to their now "official" family. Jaclyn knew he didn't really take life seriously while they were dating, but she assumed that his decision to make a life-long commitment and start a family was a good indicator that he was ready to put his boyish ways behind him.

Jaclyn begins to nag Eric about how he spends his time and Eric's response usually revolves around a "this is just who I am" mentality. The more she complains, the more Eric seems to distance himself from her. And the longer she thinks about his immaturity, the more resentful she becomes and the more she vents about him to her friends and family. At least there is one thing they can agree on: they were far happier before they got married.

#COUNTERCULTURE

It's true that our spouses should appreciate us without any expectation that we should or will ever be any different. However, our culture has distorted this concept as a defense to justify why we shouldn't have to change for anyone, including our spouse. Yet, at the same time, we expect our spouses to behave in ways that are contrary to "who they are". So it seems we have a double-standard. If we "counter" this standard, you get a much more Biblical approach: appreciate your spouse without expecting them to change, but be willing to change who you are for the betterment of your marriage. If both spouses live off of this mindset, you'll both meet somewhere blissfully in the middle.

1. AVOIDING CHANGE

Stop making _____ - most of the time, we make excuses because we are refusing to change

Change is a sign of _____ - we should allow God to transform us into the person He calls us to be

Don't be so set in who you think you are that you refuse to let God mold you into who He created you to be.

2. DON'T EXPECT CHANGE

Expecting _____ - love and accept your spouse just the way they are without any expectation of change

You can only change _____ - if you approach your marriage with the expectation that you can change your

      spouse, you will be disappointed daily

Two _____ do not make a right - if you are excusing yourself from being a better husband/wife because

      your spouse is not a good husband/wife, you are just as much to blame

> *"You, therefore, have no excuse, you who pass judgment on someone else, for*
> *at whatever point you judge another, you are condemning yourself, because you who pass*
> *judgment do the same things."-Romans 2:1 (NIV)*

God calls us to be _____-_____ - if our spouse doesn't behave the way we desire, we should

continue to serve them as the husband/wife God has called us to be with even greater fervency

Your spouse cannot be _____ for you - it is unrealistic for your spouse to be everything for you all the time

3. FOCUS ON THE GOOD STUFF

Dwell on their good _____ - there is ALWAYS something you can appreciate about your spouse,

choose to constantly think and talk about those things

> "Finally, brothers and sisters, whatever is true, whatever is noble, whatever is right,
> whatever is pure, whatever is lovely, whatever is admirable - if ANYTHING is excellent or
> praiseworthy - think about such things." - Philippians 4:8 (NIV)

Stop _____ - stop thinking or talking about all the things you don't like about your spouse or

you wish they would change

> "Watch the way you talk. Let nothing foul or dirty come out of your mouth. Say only what
> helps, each word a gift...Make a clean break with all cutting, backbiting, profane talk. Be
> gentle with one another, sensitive. Forgive one another as quickly and thoroughly as God in
> Christ forgave you." -Ephesians 4:29, 31 (MSG)

Appreciate that they are _____ - if your spouse was just like you, then they wouldn't need you to

complete them or balance them out

4. METHODS OF APPRECIATION

_____ them - no matter how seemingly insignificant, if you think of something you like about your

spouse, immediately call them, text them, post on their wall, send a carrier pigeon, etc.

Tell _____ - brag on your spouse to your friends, your family, on social media accounts, let the world

know how great they are

Respect them - it's not just about saying how much you appreciate them, but how you _____ them

_____ them - create less work for them to do

Make sure they _____ appreciated!

Appreciating your spouse doesn't just benefit your marriage because you are making them feel good about themselves. Whatever opinions of your spouse you choose to verbalize on a regular basis will either reaffirm or slowly change your true opinion of them. So in essence, you can create the spouse you have through the opinions you choose to express about them.

#DISCUSSION

Write your opinions for each question below or discuss your answers with your group/spouse.

QUESTION 1

Go back and review the #culture story on page 67. What are the long-term effects of how Eric and Jaclyn handled their situation? In light of the information given in this session, discuss how each of them should have reacted differently.

_____

_____

_____

_____

_____

QUESTION 2

Why do you think it's so easy for us to put the blame on our spouses instead of taking responsibility for our own actions?

_____

_____

_____

_____

QUESTION 3

When we do not feel that our spouse is holding up their end of the bargain, it can feel like we are reinforcing their "bad" behavior by continuing to better ourselves while they make no effort to change. Play out different methods of handling situations when your spouse is not living up to your expectations. Which one gets you to the results you are looking for?

_____

_____

_____

_____

QUESTION 4

What are some ways that we set ourselves up for disappointment when we expect our spouse to be God for us?

_____

_____

_____

_____

_____

#SELFEVALUATIONS

Score each statement on a scale of 0-5 (0=Disagree; 5=Agree). Each spouse should complete their evaluation page privately, then share and discuss their results together afterwards.

HUSBANDS: EVALUATE YOURSELF

☐ I regularly take responsibility for the behavior that I do wrong in disagreements with my wife.

☐ I do not neglect my responsibilities as a husband even if I do not feel that my wife is holding up her end of the bargain.

☐ I do not nag or try to "force" my wife to change her behavior (even if I am right).

☐ When my wife demonstrates behavior that I do not agree with, although I may bring it to her attention, I continue to love and serve her as her husband and pray and trust God to change them.

☐ I focus more on my wife's positive traits than on their negative traits.

☐ I show my wife appreciation for something (no matter how small) that she does on a daily basis in a way that makes her feel appreciated.

☐ I do not rely on my wife to "be God" for me by expecting her to make me happy constantly, be flawless or never make mistakes.

☐ My Total

HUSBANDS: EVALUATE YOUR WIFE

☐ My wife regularly takes responsibility for the behavior that she does wrong in disagreements with me.

☐ My wife does not neglect her responsibilities as a wife even if she does not feel that I am holding up my end of the bargain.

☐ My wife does not nag or try to "force" me to change my behavior (even if she is right).

☐ When I demonstrate behavior that my wife does not agree with, although she may bring it to my attention, she continues to love and serve me as my wife and pray and trust God to change me.

☐ My wife focuses more on my positive traits than on my negative traits.

☐ My wife shows me appreciation for something (no matter how small) that I do on a daily basis in a way that I feel appreciated.

☐ My wife does not rely on me to "be God" for her by expecting me to make her happy constantly, be flawless or never make mistakes.

☐ My Total

LIST 5 THINGS YOU APPRECIATE ABOUT YOUR WIFE

_____

_____

WIVES: EVALUATE YOURSELF

☐ I regularly take responsibility for the behavior that I do wrong in disagreements with my husband.

☐ I do not neglect my responsibilities as a wife even if I do not feel that my husband is holding up his end of the bargain.

☐ I do not nag or try to "force" my husband to change his behavior (even if I am right).

☐ When my husband demonstrates behavior that I do not agree with, although I may bring it to his attention, I continue to love and serve him as his wife and pray and trust God to change them.

☐ I focus more on my husband's positive traits than on his negative traits.

☐ I show my husband appreciation for something (no matter how small) that they do on a daily basis in a way that makes him feel appreciated.

☐ I do not rely on my husband to "be God" for me by expecting him to make me happy constantly, be flawless or never make mistakes.

☐ My Total

WIVES: EVALUATE YOUR HUSBAND

☐ My husband regularly takes responsibility for the behavior that he does wrong in disagreements with me.

☐ My husband does not neglect his responsibilities as a husband even if he does not feel that I am holding up my end of the bargain.

☐ My husband does not nag or try to "force" me to change my behavior (even if he is right).

☐ When I demonstrate behavior that my husband does not agree with, although he may bring it to my attention, he continues to love and serve me as my husband and pray and trust God to change me.

☐ My husband focuses more on my positive traits than on my negative traits.

☐ My husband shows me appreciation for something (no matter how small) that I do on a daily basis in a way that makes me feel appreciated.

☐ My husband does not rely on me to "be God" for him by expecting me to make him happy constantly, be flawless or never make mistakes.

☐ My Total Score

LIST 5 THINGS YOU APPRECIATE ABOUT YOUR HUSBAND

_____

_____

HOW HEALTHY ARE THE EXPECTATIONS AND APPRECIATION IN YOUR MARRIAGE?
(add your total + your spouse's total)

Combined Total: 54-70	Less is more!
Combined Total: 36-53	Great expectations.
Combined Total: 18-35	Suffering from a little appreciation depletion?
Combined Total: 0-17	Expect more, pay less

INTIMATE APPAREL

#sex #romance

#culture
"I'm also interested in the modern suggestion that you can have a
combination of love and sex in a marriage - which no previous society has ever believed."
@Alain De Botton

#CULTURE

Clay wants sex all the time - Amy, not so much. At the beginning of their relationship, Clay's sexual advances used to make Amy feel special, but now they just make her feel annoyed and slightly used. This goes way over Clay's head, after all, what more could Amy want than to know that he desires to be with her sexually? On the other hand, amidst all the sexual advances, the last thing Amy is feeling from Clay is special.

Despite Amy's annoyance and opinions that sex shouldn't be so important and such a consuming element in Clay's life, she doesn't hesitate to use his desire for sex to her advantage. If she wants to buy a dress that they don't have money for - she just offers sex. If he does something that makes her mad - she punishes him with no sex. The scarcity of regular sexual activity in their marriage, makes Amy's use of sex a very effective bargaining tool. This setup seems profitable to both parties for awhile. However, at the end of the day, neither Clay nor Amy feel like they are getting what they really want in the sex and romance department.

#COUNTERCULTURE

1. SEX MISCONCEPTION #1: SEX ENDS AFTER MARRIAGE

It's said often that sex ends after marriage and that romance is dead. But God intends for the contrary to happen in your marriage! The Song of Solomon depicts a marriage that is not only filled with a vibrant and adventurous sex life, but also a marriage that is brimming with the sweet scents of romance.

Your _____ life is usually a good indicator of the _____ of your marriage.

An individual who feels sexually _____ by their spouse (i.e. she is proactive in initiating sex), will also

grow in _____ in other areas of their life.

What's acceptable? Any sexual activity that is _____ done between a consenting husband and his

consenting wife _____ that is not _____ or illegal is probably acceptable.

Sexual intimacy in the right context is a form of spiritual expression and praise towards God.

2. SEX MISCONCEPTION #2: SEX IS JUST PHYSICAL

> "It's good for a man to have a wife, and for a woman to have a husband. Sexual drives are strong, but marriage is strong enough to contain them and provide for a balanced and fulfilling sexual life in a world of sexual disorder. The marriage bed must be a place of mutuality - the husband seeking to satisfy his wife, the wife seeking to satisfy her husband."
> - I Corinthians 7:2-3 (MSG)

Healthy sex represents the _____ and _____ relationship that should be reflected in a healthy marriage.

Great sex comes from a great _____ and a great friendship comes from a deep connection and a

deep connection comes from a willingness to _____ yourself.

Sex is meant to be a tool to keep your sexual desires _____ exclusively on your spouse. Outside

influences, such as porn, distort your focus to be directly on sex, which drives you away from your

spouse _____, _____ and _____.

3. SEX MISCONCEPTION #3: SEX IS JUST A TOOL

Sex is a _____ that each spouse holds for the other to remind them how _____ they are.

Sex should be given freely to your spouse without_____ or _____.

> "Marriage is not a place to "stand up for your rights." Marriage is a decision to serve the other,
> whether in bed or out. Abstaining from sex is permissible for a period of time if you both
> agree to it, and if it's for the purposes of prayer and fasting - but only for such times. Then
> come back together again. Satan has an ingenious way to tempting us when we least expect
> it. I'm not, understand, commanding these periods of abstinence - only providing my best
> counsel if you should choose them." - I Corinthians 7:4-6 (MSG)

God created parts of our anatomy to have no other purpose except for _____.

4. ROMANCE MISCONCEPTION #1: "I DON'T HAVE ENOUGH MONEY TO BE ROMANTIC"

> "As a loving hind and a graceful doe, let her breasts satisfy you at all times; be exhilarated
> always with her love." -Proverbs 5:19 (NASB)

Romance - Anything that makes your _____ feel _____.

5. ROMANCE MISCONCEPTION #2: ROMANCE IS A TOOL TO GET THEM "IN THE MOOD"

Romance might get your spouse in the _____, but if you do something romantic for the

_____ of getting them in the mood, it's no longer considered romance - just deceptive.

6. ROMANCE MISCONCEPTION #3: SEX IS ROMANTIC

Romance requires that you don't make your spouse feel like they are the only _____, but that if you

were given all the _____ in the world, they are the only one you would ever want to be with.

7. SEX & ROMANCE MISCONCEPTION #4:
DOING SOMETHNG ROMANTIC IS THE SAME THING AS BEING ROMANTIC

If you are only doing exactly what your spouse _____ of you, then it feels more like _____ than

romance. In order to satsify your spouse sexually and romantically, requires more than simply going

through the motions.

#DISCUSSION
Write your opinions for each question below or discuss your answers with your group/spouse.

QUESTION 1
Go back and review the #culture story on page 75. What are the long-term effects of how Clay and Amy handled their situation? In light of the information given in this session, discuss how each of them should have reacted differently.

QUESTION 2
What are some reasons that sex and romance fall low on the priority list and what can a husband or wife do to make those things a higher priority?

QUESTION 3
How does porn, either outside of the marriage or viewed together as a couple, negatively affect your sex life?

QUESTION 4
What are some things that your spouse can do that make you feel special? Some things they do that don't make you feel special?

#SELFEVALUATIONS
Score each statement on a scale of 0-5 (0=Disagree; 5=Agree).

Each spouse should complete their evaluation page privately,
then share and discuss their results together afterwards.

HUSBANDS: EVALUATE YOURSELF

☐ I am satisfied with the amount of sex and romance in my marriage.

☐ I make a proactive effort to have sex with my spouse and not just when they ask.

☐ I do not engage in external sexual pleasure (affairs, porn, romance novels, etc) outside of or as a part of my marriage relationship.

☐ I do not use sex as a bargaining tool or withhold sex when I'm mad.

☐ I make my spouse feel special.

☐ If I do something sweet or thoughtful for my spouse, I do it because I love them, not because I want to get them "in the mood."

☐ I have a great friendship and a deep connection with my spouse aside from our sex life.

☐ My Total

HUSBANDS: EVALUATE YOUR WIFE

☐ My spouse is satisfied with the amount of sex and romance in our marriage.

☐ My spouse makes a proactive effort to have sex with me and not just when I ask.

☐ My spouse does not engage in external sexual pleasure (affairs, porn, romance novels, etc) outside of or as a part of our marriage relationship.

☐ My spouse does not use sex as a bargaining tool or withhold sex when they are mad.

☐ My spouse makes me feel special.

☐ If my spouse does something sweet or thoughtful for me, they do it because they love me, not because they want to get me "in the mood."

☐ My spouse has a great friendship and a deep connection with me aside from our sex life.

☐ My Spouse's Total

WIVES: EVALUATE YOURSELF

☐ I am satisfied with the amount of sex and romance in my marriage.

☐ I make a proactive effort to have sex with my spouse and not just when they ask.

☐ I do not engage in external sexual pleasure (affairs, porn, romance novels, etc) outside of or as a part of my marriage relationship.

☐ I do not use sex as a bargaining tool or withhold sex when I'm mad.

☐ I make my spouse feel special.

☐ If I do something sweet or thoughtful for my spouse, I do it because I love them, not because I want to get them "in the mood."

☐ I have a great friendship and a deep connection with my spouse aside from our sex life.

☐ My Total

WIVES: EVALUATE YOUR HUSBAND

☐ My spouse is satisfied with the amount of sex and romance in our marriage.

☐ My spouse makes a proactive effort to have sex with me and not just when I ask.

☐ My spouse does not engage in external sexual pleasure (affairs, porn, romance novels, etc) outside of or as a part of our marriage relationship.

☐ My spouse does not use sex as a bargaining tool or withhold sex when they are mad.

☐ My spouse makes me feel special.

☐ If my spouse does something sweet or thoughtful for me, they do it because they love me, not because they want to get me "in the mood."

☐ My spouse has a great friendship and a deep connection with me aside from our sex life.

☐ My Spouse's Total

HOW HEALTHY IS THE SEX & ROMANCE IN YOUR MARRIAGE?
(add your total + your spouse's total)

Combined Total: 54-70   Lace and Stringy Things
Combined Total: 36-53   Slips of Silk
Combined Total: 18-35   Flannel Pajamas
Combined Total: 0-17   Bathrobes & Muumuus

WHAT'S LOVE GOT TO DO WITH IT?

#lust #love

#culture
"Follow your heart."
@most everyone everywhere

#CULTURE

Jason and Erica have been married for several years. In the last few years, Jason has become unloving and critical of Erica. Although Jason doesn't believe it has anything to do with it, Erica feels that his heightened attention to porn has left their marriage feeling distant. Thankfully, Erica has found support from her best friend, Nick. Nick and Erica have been best friends for most of their lives. Although they lost touch when Erica first got married, she's glad they reconnected and have picked up right where they left off.

As time goes on, Jason, although he insists that he is doing nothing wrong (after all, "every" guy looks at porn), continues to hide the amount of time he spends with porn. Erica, although she insists that "nothing is going on", begins to hide her activities and text messages with Nick. Erica feels secure and safe with Nick and Nick loves how much Erica has started to depend on him and admire him. One day, Erica realizes that her soul-mate has been by her side nearly her entire life and she never knew it and now that she's found him, he takes her breathe away - literally, and of course, Nick feels the same way.

She makes the decision to tell Jason that she's "fallen out of love" with him and the chemistry between them just isn't there anymore and she wants a divorce. Because Erica never physically cheated on Jason, the divorce process is mutual and amiable. They both agree that any love they once had for each other has simply faded away.

Once the divorce is finalized, Jason takes advantage of his new found freedom and Nick and Erica ride off into the sunset. After a few years, Jason settles down with a girl who can really connect with him and doesn't yet know about his porn addiction (or just doesn't care - yet). Overtime, Nick and Erica's marriage becomes more routine, and although they really love each other and Nick is a great husband to Erica, things just aren't as passionate as they used to be. Erica's life seems perfect, but lacks zeal and excitement...until she meets Carlos, a new co-worker she's been assigned to train at work...

#COUNTERCULTURE

We are a society driven by our emotions. Our culture determines what the "right" decision is based on how we feel instead of what God states to be true in His Word. We live for the next emotional high - whether in a movie, someone else's life or our own life. The dependence many of us have on our emotions to make us feel "alive" has sadly left behind a trail of broken homes and broken people in it's wake. God's intention for us is not to live in a passionless marriage in our lifeless existence. Our emotions are a gift from God to give our lives color, but we must learn to control them and give them boundaries so they are used to create a masterpiece instead of a splattered mess.

1. DEFINING OURSELVES

We are made up of three parts: _____, _____ and _____.

Likewise, we relate to others in three ways:

_____ (body) - a response to someone that can be detected in a measurable, phsyical sense "chemistry"

_____ (soul) - a connection to someone mentally through our mind, will and emotions "soul tie"

_____ (spirit) - when we selflessly care about someone's well-being "love"

2. LUST

Lust - a romantic attraction to someone that is so intense that you can feel it _____ (sweaty palms,

butterflies, "falling in love", etc)

Lust is an _____ - based experience with no weight given to reality, consequences or morality

> *"The heart is more deceitful than anything else. And is desperately sick;*
> *who can understand it?" -Jeremiah 17:9 (NASB)*

The fact that we are feeling consumed with an _____ has very little to do with whether or not those

feelings are _____.

3. LOVE

Where lust leaves us unsatisfied and constantly wanting for more, love leaves us feeling satisfied and fulfilled.

Love - _____-_____ commitment to someone that trumps any conflicting emotions

> *"Love is patient, love is kind. It does not envy, it does not boast, it is not proud. It does not*
> *dishonor others, it is not self-seeking, it is not easily angered, it keeps no record of wrongs.*
> *Love does not delight in evil but rejoices with the truth. It always protects, always trusts, always*
> *hopes, always perseveres." -I Corinthians 13:4-7 (NIV)*

Love is not an _____ - it's a selfless command

4. BUILDING A MARRIAGE ON LOVE

_____ your heart - the best way to prevent yourself from having to battle with the wrong emotions

is to prevent yourself from developing those emotions to begin with

_____ your emotions - your emotions have limitations, you must choose carefully where you are

pouring your emotions into and from where you are receiving your emotional needs

5. GETTING YOURSELF OUT OF A PIT

If you find yourself with misplaced emotions, _____ it or admit it, _____ whatever fuels

the misplaced emotions, _____ your attention and your emotions in the right things and finally

_____ your heart moving forward.

If marriage is just about "being in love" and making us happy, we'd have to get a new marriage every 2-3 years,
but God has called us to be committed to our spouses through every season, regardless of how we may feel.

#DISCUSSION
Write your opinions for each question below or discuss your answers with your group/spouse.

QUESTION 1
Go back and review the #culture story on page 83. What are the long-term effects of how Jason and Erica handled their situation? In light of the information given in this session, discuss how each of them should have reacted differently.

QUESTION 2
How has our culture (especially in media) created an illusion of what love is and how is this illusion destructive to our lives?

QUESTION 3
A common word of advice given in our culture is "just follow your heart." What are some situations in your marriage when this is not Godly advice?

QUESTION 4
What are some common ways that couples deal with a loss of emotions towards their spouse as their marriages grow more routine? How should they respond?

#SELFEVALUATIONS
Score each statement on a scale of 0-5 (0=Disagree; 5=Agree).

Each spouse should complete their evaluation page privately,
then share and discuss their results together afterwards.

HUSBANDS: EVALUATE YOURSELF

◻ I understand the difference between lust and love.

◻ I am not currently pouring any of my emotions into something or someone else such as porn, scripted dramas (novels, TV, movies), a friend of the opposite sex, fantasies, etc.

◻ Even during the times that I may not feel like I am "in love" with my spouse, I am still 100% committed to them.

◻ I understand that I can control how I feel, even if it doesn't happen instantly.

◻ I understand that my emotions are desperately misleading and deceptive and I do not make decisions based on feelings alone, but look to God's Word for direction.

◻ I am careful to guard my emotions so that I am never in a situation where I can develop inappropriate affections for someone or something.

◻ I strive to demonstrate the fruits of love as explained in I Corinthians 13.

◻ My Total

HUSBANDS: EVALUATE YOUR WIFE

◻ My spouse understands the difference between lust and love.

◻ My spouse is not currently pouring any of their emotions into something or someone else such as porn, scripted dramas (novels, TV, movies), a friend of the opposite sex, fantasies, etc.

◻ Even during the times that they may not feel like they are "in love" with me, my spouse is still 100% committed to me.

◻ My spouse understands that they can control how they feel, even if it doesn't happen instantly.

◻ My spouse understands that their emotions are desperately misleading and deceptive and they do not make decisions based on feelings alone, but look to God's Word for direction.

◻ My spouse is careful to guard their emotions so that they are never in a situation where they can develop inappropriate affections for someone or something.

◻ My spouse strives to demonstrate the fruits of love as explained in I Corinthians 13.

◻ My Spouse's Total

WIVES: EVALUATE YOURSELF

☐ I understand the difference between lust and love.

☐ I am not currently pouring any of my emotions into something or someone else such as porn, scripted dramas (novels, TV, movies), a friend of the opposite sex, fantasies, etc.

☐ Even during the times that I may not feel like I am "in love" with my spouse, I am still 100% committed to them.

☐ I understand that I can control how I feel, even if it doesn't happen instantly.

☐ I understand that my emotions are desperately misleading and deceptive and I do not make decisions based on feelings alone, but look to God's Word for direction.

☐ I am careful to guard my emotions so that I am never in a situation where I can develop inappropriate affections for someone or something.

☐ I strive to demonstrate the fruits of love as explained in I Corinthians 13.

☐ My Total

WIVES: EVALUATE YOUR HUSBAND

☐ My spouse understands the difference between lust and love.

☐ My spouse is not currently pouring any of their emotions into something or someone else such as porn, scripted dramas (novels, TV, movies), a friend of the opposite sex, fantasies, etc.

☐ Even during the times that they may not feel like they are "in love" with me, my spouse is still 100% committed to me.

☐ My spouse understands that they can control how they feel, even if it doesn't happen instantly.

☐ My spouse understands that their emotions are desperately misleading and deceptive and they do not make decisions based on feelings alone, but look to God's Word for direction.

☐ My spouse is careful to guard their emotions so that they are never in a situation where they can develop inappropriate affections for someone or something.

☐ My spouse strives to demonstrate the fruits of love as explained in I Corinthians 13.

☐ My Spouse's Total

HOW HEALTHY IS THE LOVE IN YOUR MARRIAGE?
(add your total + your spouse's total)

Combined Total: 54-70   Happily in love!
Combined Total: 36-53   Falling....in love
Combined Total: 18-35   Wearing your heart on your sleeve again?
Combined Total: 0-17   Time for a heart-to-heart.

YOU + ME = ONE

#commitment

#culture
"I've never been married, but I tell people I'm divorced
so they won't think something's wrong with me."
@Elayne Boosler

#CULTURE

Sean spends the Saturday hanging with the guys while Abby cleans the house before she schedules an outing with a few of her girlfriends. After a long day, they are both spent and head to bed. When the week starts up again, Sean and Abby both go to their respective jobs and have their own separate plans in the evening. The only time Sean and Abby talk are when they are coordinating the bills (which requires very little discussion since they've had the same setup for their finances for several years) or discussing necessary errands or appearances that must be made by the other person. Family dinners are pretty much obsolete since their children started driving and everything else in their life is pretty routine.

Although their life and marriage seems to be absent of any major conflicts, there isn't a lot of interaction happening between them - and definitely not due to a shortage of topics of conversation. Sean has been contemplating putting in for a promotion at work, his dad has recently started undergoing chemotherapy and the guys are trying to convince him to go-in with them on a new ski boat. Abby's life seems just as active: she's thinking of taking some art classes, planning on stealing away a week to go on a girl's getaway cruise in the next month and currently consoling her best friend as she goes through a messy divorce. None of these topics have been mentioned between the two of them and there haven't been any discussion on the decisions that need to be made or the emotional burdens that each of them are feeling.

Somewhere throughout the years - between having kids early on and all the drama that came with them - Sean and Abby drifted apart and became content living their own individual lives as comfortable roommates. Although life seems to be missing "spice", they both relish the applause and admiration of their friends for the longevity of their marriage.

#COUNTERCULTURE

Doing marriage the way God intended goes beyond just staying married. It's not enough to just not be divorced. God desires to use our marriage to propel us into His perfect will for our lives. Separating ourselves from our spouse, whether legally or by a discorded lifestyle, delays His ultimate purpose for us as individuals. If we choose to put obedience to God above our own personal happiness, then God is faithful to give us the happiness we were seeking in the first place.

1. LIVING AS ONE

> *"For this reason a man shall leave his father and mother, and the two shall become ONE*
> *FLESH; so they are no longer two, but ONE FLESH." -Mark 10:7-8 (NASB)*

"One" - _____ +   "Flesh" - _____ _____

        = A _____ _____ _____

> *"The wife does not have authority over her own body, but the husband does; and likewise also*
> *the husband does not have authority over his own body, but the wife does."*
> *-I Corinthians 7:4 (NASB)*

We are no longer to live _____ lives while trying to _____ each other. We are now

        commanded to live _____ life, together.

Appreciate your _____ - your spouse's differences is what balances you out so that your "one flesh"

can be a perfect entity

_____ Together - adopt your spouse's dream as your own dream

_____ your Steps - make no decisions without the knowledge and agreement of your spouse

Keep in _____ - make contact with your spouse several times a day, however you can (call, text, hug, kiss, etc)

Put yourself _____ _____ - for the greater good of the whole, make yourself more vulnerable by living a

life that's totally exposed and held accountable by your spouse

Disagree with _____ - view your arguments as an opportunity to grow closer together, not draw you apart

2. COMMITMENT

Stay _____ - a singular living organism cannot be torn apart without causing near irreparable damage

to both parts

God hates _____ - God doesn't hate you, but He hates divorce because of what it does to His creation

> "'I hate divorce,' says the God of Israel. God of the Angel Armies says, 'I hate the violent
> dismembering of the 'one flesh' of marriage...'" -Malachi 2:16 (MSG)

3. RESTORATION

Each Season _____ - the season you are in right now is not permanent

Be _____ - don't just seek God's hand - but seek His face through prayer, learning and obedience

Be "all-in" - our relationship with God is about _____, _____ and _____ ,

not abandonment - our marriages should reflect these same traits

Nothing is _____ - God can use your failures to strengthen your marriage

4. A GREATER PURPOSE

Grow _____ to God - the more you grow in your relationship with God, the more He molds your character

and the better spouse you become

God uses your marriage to transform you as an _____ and your marriage is directly tied to

your God-given _____.

#DISCUSSION

Write your opinions for each question below or discuss your answers with your group/spouse.

QUESTION 1

Go back and review the #culture story on page 91. What are the long-term effects of how Sean and Abby handled their situation? In light of the information given in this session, discuss how each of them should have reacted differently.

QUESTION 2

What are some common examples of married couples not living as "one" being? What are the negative consequences that can result from the mindset that allows each individual to operate and live individually within the marriage?

QUESTION 3

Our marriage should be a reflection of God's love for the world, what are some ways that your marriage is or can be a reflection of God's relationship with mankind?

QUESTION 4

Christians have a tendency to say they believe that God is powerful enough to provide financially or keep them out of hell, but when it comes to believing that God is powerful enough to heal their marriage or transform their spouse (or themselves), all of a sudden, they feel that task is too big for God. Why is that and how do we change that perspective in ourselves?

#SELFEVALUATIONS

Score each statement on a scale of 0-5 (0=Disagree; 5=Agree).

Each spouse should complete their evaluation page privately,
then share and discuss their results together afterwards.

HUSBANDS: EVALUATE YOURSELF

☐ When considering decisions and making plans, I always consider both my spouse and I, not just myself.

☐ I align my vision with my spouses' vision so we can operate in unity (whether that vision be a dream, decision, goal, etc)

☐ There is nothing that my spouse intentionally does not know about me, my feelings, my struggles or my opinions.

☐ If there is something interesting that happens during my day, my spouse is the first person I want to tell.

☐ I am committed to standing beside my spouse regardless of the circumstances. I am committed beyond just staying legally married.

☐ I make it a habit to extend grace and forgiveness to my spouse and do not hold bitterness or resentment against them.

☐ I am continually growing in my relationship with God.

☐ My Total

HUSBANDS: EVALUATE YOUR WIFE

☐ When considering decisions and making plans, my spouse always considers both themselves and me, not just them.

☐ My spouse aligns their vision with my vision so we can operate in unity (whether that vision be a dream, decision, goal, etc)

☐ I feel that there is nothing that I do not know about my spouse, their feelings, their struggles or their opinions.

☐ If there is something interesting that happens during my spouses' day, I am the first person they want to tell.

☐ My spouse is committed to standing beside me regardless of the circumstances. They are committed beyond just staying legally married.

☐ My spouse makes it a habit to extend grace and forgiveness to me and does not hold bitterness or resentment against me.

☐ My spouse is continually growing in their relationship with God.

☐ My Spouse's Total

WIVES: EVALUATE YOURSELF

☐ When considering decisions and making plans, I always consider both my spouse and I, not just myself.

☐ I align my vision with my spouses' vision so we can operate in unity (whether that vision be a dream, decision, goal, etc)

☐ There is nothing that my spouse intentionally does not know about me, my feelings, my struggles or my opinions.

☐ If there is something interesting that happens during my day, my spouse is the first person I want to tell.

☐ I am committed to standing beside my spouse regardless of the circumstances. I am committed beyond just staying legally married.

☐ I make it a habit to extend grace and forgiveness to my spouse and do not hold bitterness or resentment against them.

☐ I am continually growing in my relationship with God.

☐ My Total

WIVES: EVALUATE YOUR HUSBAND

☐ When considering decisions and making plans, my spouse always considers both themselves and me, not just them.

☐ My spouse aligns their vision with my vision so we can operate in unity (whether that vision be a dream, decision, goal, etc)

☐ I feel that there is nothing that I do not know about my spouse, their feelings, their struggles or their opinions.

☐ If there is something interesting that happens during my spouses' day, I am the first person they want to tell.

☐ My spouse is committed to standing beside me regardless of the circumstances. They are committed beyond just staying legally married.

☐ My spouse makes it a habit to extend grace and forgiveness to me and does not hold bitterness or resentment against me.

☐ My spouse is continually growing in their relationship with God.

☐ My Spouse's Total

HOW HEALTHY IS THE COMMITMENT IN YOUR MARRIAGE?
(add your total + your spouse's total)

Combined Total: 54-70	Two peas in a pod!
Combined Total: 36-53	You're like peanut butter & jelly.
Combined Total: 18-35	Merging road ahead.
Combined Total: 0-17	Please reconnect.

LEADER NOTES

answer key and sample discussion answers

SESSION 1: THE BUSINESS OF MARRIAGE

FILL-IN-THE-BLANK
covenant
1. relearn, reengage, redate, reimagine
2. laugh, happy, Biblical, attainable, inapplicable
3. perspective, Trust
4. valleys

QUESTION 1
The Results: Vanessa's persistence in trying to "fix" her marriage may actually end up doing more harm than good. She has become so wrapped up in controlling the situation that she has forgotten that marriage is not about "being perfect" but about loving your spouse. The more Vanessa pushes, the further away Drew gets until eventually, despite Vanessa's intentions, their marriage becomes another cliche joke in the guy's locker room.

Drew: Instead of letting Vanessa take the reins unhindered, perhaps Drew should try talking to Vanessa about her obsession with trying to be perfect. If she still doesn't get it, Drew could try unique ways to reconnect with Vanessa...write a note, surprise her with flowers at work, have dinner ready for her when she gets home...the possibilities are endless. Although Drew seems to be on the passive end of the situation, there is usually something he can do to better the situation.

Vanessa: Trying to make a better marriage is great...however, if the only "problem" is that there doesn't seem to be an existing friendship anymore, Vanessa may need to put aside all the workbooks and take Drew out to a football game or sit down with him when he is doing something he deems "fun" and take an interest in his interest. These things may seem menial, but it creates a habit on a casual level of doing things together and talking together. This habit of "togetherness" will eventually resurface when it's necessary to handle more serious issues in their marriage.

QUESTION 2
Personal answers. Couples don't live in their "honeymoon stage' forever because they get sidetracked with their own agendas and interests and lose sight of caring about their spouse. They also forget to continue to enjoy each other's company while they are in the pursuit of taking care of all their responsibilities.

QUESTION 3
Stress and obligations certainly distract you from being able to enjoy time with your spouse. However, the trials of life are much easier to get through when you and your spouse are able to rely and work through things together. A good place to begin "teaming up" with your spouse is to connect over something else besides "business". Even if your leisure interests may not be similar, take turns enjoying activities that your spouse enjoys. If you are able to connect and communicate over something casual, it will help open the door to work together and communicate about things that are of a more serious nature. Also, don't be afraid to talk about each other's dreams. Don't get so wrapped up in everything that happens today that you forget to have vision and dreams for what you hope God will do through your life.

QUESTION 4
When we take life too seriously or try to fix things ourselves, it's usually because we are trying to take control of the situation rather than relying on God's provision. Our first priority should be to grow in our love and relationship with God and then to love and care about our spouse (and what they love and care about). As we grow and walk in obedience, we need to trust that God will lead us in the right direction. We should try to be content with wherever God wants us to be - whether that be in your mom's garage or at a job you gravely dislike - and trust that God has a plan. Do the best you can with what you are given right now and then count your blessings and enjoy the journey. Be careful not to be so consumed and distracted with things that will not matter when you leave this world.

SESSION 2: WHAT WOMEN WANT

FILL-IN-THE-BLANK
1. respected, esteemed, successful, secure, loved, fear, doubt
2. Christ, church
3. Spiritual, loves, trust, obedient, Emotional, trustworthy, heart, Physical, physical, self-sacrifice
4. Admiration, dwell, Praise, compliment, lead, respect, final, respect, confidence, deserve, commanded

QUESTION 1
The Results: Nadia never got the emotional security she really wanted from Philip after confiding in him. Additionally, all the negative comments Philip heard Nadia relay to her best friend cut-away from the respect that Philip needed from Nadia. The family drama wasn't resolved either, so this same cycle would repeat itself the next time a situation occurred. Eventually, resentment and bitterness could build up and drive Philip and Nadia apart.

Philip: There are a few different ways that this situation could have been handled. After being confronted with the situation, Philip should have decided to PROTECT Nadia from these attacks either indirectly by advising Nadia to block them from her social media accounts and reaffirming her position in his life or protected her directly by respectfully confronting his mother and sister and reaffirming her position in his life to them and asking them to stop attacking Nadia. Once married, your spouse becomes your first and most important human relationship. Genesis 2:24 states "Therefore a man shall leave his father and mother and be joined to his wife, and they shall become one flesh."

Nadia: In Nadia's case, she should be willing to take whatever protective advise Philip offers – allowing him to lead. If he doesn't offer to protect her, she might consider suggesting to him that he take one of the steps above – not demanding it – suggesting it. If he is still unwilling to protect her indirectly or directly, Nadia should "encourage herself in the Lord" and pray about her situation. If she needs to speak to a friend or counselor, she should do so - but in no circumstance should she relay insults of her husband to someone else or dwell on his negative traits.

QUESTION 2
Sample Answer: Society is on a kick to empower women and emasculate men: feminists demand equality, independence and respect and men are expected to be lazy and disconnected (except when it comes to sex). The world believes that a desired setup in marriage is one in which women get to rule the house (no matter how false their sense of security may be) and men find it necessary to lie to their wives so they can continue "flying under the radar" and do what they want without "hurting" their marriage.

In reality, the way God intends marriages to operate is usually the exact opposite of what culture teaches us. A wife that refuses to allow her husband to "protect" her and refuses to respect the position of leadership that her husband holds will soon find herself miserable and unfulfilled in her marriage. This leads her to progressively disrespect her husband even more until eventually she finds him worthless and wants to leave the him. A husband who consistently refuses to take responsibility in securing his wife spiritually, emotionally and physically will find himself with a wife that grows more bitter over time and gradually increases in her disrespect for him until he either completely submits to her for the remainder of their marriage or finally decides that he desires to be treated with some respect and wants to leave the marriage.

In the end, one of the greatest attacks on marriages today is the deception of what men and women TRULY want from each other. As we can see, if husbands and wives were to get what culture says they want, it would lead them directly to the destruction of their marriage and a heart full of bitterness and emptiness. Women need to respect their husbands (demonstrated by submission) in order for their husbands to provide security and husbands need to provide security for their wives (demonstrated by leadership) in order for their wives to respect them. It has to start somewhere.

QUESTION 3
Sample Answers: Husbands will not take on the leadership role, wives feel their husbands must "earn" their respect, wives begin to point out their husband's flaws more than focusing on their good qualities, etc.

Regardless of how legitimate a wife's reasoning may be, it's important for them to show their husbands respect, whether they have earned it or not.

QUESTION 4
Sample Answers: There is no reason to protect someone (wife) who doesn't need it (because they are independent and take control of the relationship), outside threats distract a husband or take priority over protecting his wife (i.e. porn destroys a wife's security, workaholics may be providing financial security but are not providing emotional security, etc), a husband is struggling with the confidence to be able to provide security because his wife refuses to encourage him and build his confidence to be able to do so, not being able to trust her husband takes away the ability for a wife to live in emotional freedom within her marriage (in this case, a husband is taking away his wife's sense of security), etc.

SESSION 3: DICTATORS

FILL-IN-THE-BLANK
1. Christ, man, wife
2. Dictator, command, submit
3. selfless, sacrifice, desires
4. Prideful, can't
5. love, servant, submit, truth, wisdom, delegate, self-esteem
6. lead, confidence, helpmate, failures

QUESTION 1
The Results: It's not difficult to see where this is going to end up. If neither party is willing to step-down from the leadership role, either they will leave the marriage or submission by one party will be forced through threats or physical abuse. And even then, neither spouse is getting what they truly desire. Regardless of who wins the battle for "head of household", the husband is still not respected and the wife is constantly living in fear or stress without anyone to lean on or protect her.

Note: Biblical leadership can not be forced or taken, there is never justification for physical abuse by either the husband or wife. If there is domestic violence taking place in your marriage, we urge you to find safety and seek professional help. Physical abuse does not mean that your marriage is beyond restoration, but it may mean you need to find somewhere free from that abuse to live while you consider your options and allow God the opportunity to heal your spouse.

Jackson: Although the concept of living carefree is appealing, eventually every man desires to be respected on some level. If Jackson desired to lead his family, he should have communicated that with love and humility to Yvonne. Then, whether or not Yvonne was open to the shift in leadership, Jackson should begin learning how to become a servant-leader and focused on his relationship with God in prayer and devotion. Leadership comes with responsibility, so if Yvonne is still unwilling to relinquish the position of "leader" in their home, Jackson should make a more diligent effort to serve and love her through pro-actively taking care of things around the house or joining in the process of family decisions. It may not happen instantly, but overtime, he will be able to regain Yvonne's trust in his ability to lead.

Yvonne: Although Yvonne feels like she wants to be in charge, the reality is probably that she doesn't necessarily want all the stress that comes with being responsible for everything, but she wants to be able to trust that someone capable is handling things. As stated in Session 2, every woman, on some level, desires to be protected and cared for....however, this simply isn't possible unless she allows Jackson to take the lead. There may be bumps along the road, but the best thing Yvonne can do for Jackson is to encourage him and help him transition into the leadership role. Ultimately, Yvonne must put her trust in God and that His ways and His methods are what work in the long run.

QUESTION 2
The enemy is not stupid....he is crafty. He understands that as long as we are not able to fulfill our God-given roles in our marriages, then our marriage is undefended against every other attack. We are surrounded by media and political movements that raise women up to be strong and independent and cast men as stupid and lazy. This feeds on the woman's misconceived desire to be in control and a man's misconceived desire to not have to be responsible for anything. No matter how much each gender desires these things, neither one of them bring us joy. At our core, men want the admiration and respect of a wife who trusts him enough to follow him (and the confidence that he can lead successfully which only comes by his following God)...this is what brings the joy that both parties are seeking. Our society has painted leadership as a chance to be a dictator and make decisions on their own without accountability and without concern for anyone else. But God created marriage to be a partnership, each person having their role in that partnership. The husband is to lead with a servant's heart...lifting his wife above his own importance. But ultimately, God has given the authority for the "final decision" to rest in the husband's hands.

QUESTION 3
When making decisions or weighing options, the husband should put his own personal (and sometimes selfish) desires aside and think about the well-being of his wife and family (financially, spiritually, mentally and physically). Often our focus is just one of those (financially) but what about the others. Would our decision change? Being the "head of the household" doesn't mean that the husband leads with no regard for his wife. Leading as a servant-leader means that he needs to discuss major decisions with his wife and truly respect and understand what she is saying before making a decision.

QUESTION 4
As best he can according to the way God has designed marriage. Our roles are not dependant on our spouses fulfilling theirs. A husband must step into his role as "head of the household" before anyone else can step out. The best place to start leading is spiritually. As his wife starts seeing him lead the family spiritually (prayer, worship, church, Bible reading), she will begin to respect his decisions in other areas. However, a husband cannot allow his wife's unwillingness to submit to be a ticket to become a General. If he becomes a LOVING leader, his wife will WANT to let him lead. He cannot force his wife to submit or make them follow his lead...they must do so on their own accord.

SESSION 4: DOORMATS

FILL-IN-THE-BLANK
1. hypotasso, arrange
2. favor, support, benefit, command
3. forced, God, servant, home
4. strengths, joy, everything
5. God, cherish, responsibility, above, need

QUESTION 1
The Results: Because of Elizabeth's naturally passive personality, it's possible that she and Davis would remain in this type of marriage contently until death. However, Davis would continue to go without the support that he so desperately needs from a partner who complements him and Elizabeth would never reach her full purpose and potential in life.

Davis: It's great that Davis is willing to shoulder the responsibility of being the head of his house and make good decisions for his family. However, he neglects to recognize that part of leading his family means recognizing his weaknesses and his wife's strengths (whether that be marketing or good-decision making) and creating an environment of respect for both parties within the marriage PARTNERSHIP. He is attempting to handle everything on his own and God didn't intend for him to do that. God provided him a wife who could support, logistically assist, encourage and challenge him. Additionally, God's purpose and calling on Elizabeth's life is no less important than Davis'. Recognizing Elizabeth's passive nature, Davis should try to be attuned when Elizabeth does mention a dream or show skill in a certain area and encourage and support Elizabeth to pursue all that God has in-store for her...even if that means that Davis would have to help out more around the house. Whatever the arrangement, it's important for Davis to understand that marriage is a partnership where both parties work together to help the other achieve what God has called them to do.

Elizabeth: There's absolutely nothing wrong with Elizabeth's desire to be stay at home and raise their children. There would also not be anything wrong with Elizabeth being the "bread-winner" and Davis being a stay-at-home dad. As these lessons indicate, the tasks that each person fulfills in the marriage is not as important as each party being able to fulfill their roles. Unfortunately, Elizabeth's desire not to be involved or burdened with the logistics of life do not fall in line with God's desire for her to be a helpmate for Davis. A helpmate is not the same as hired-help. Hired-help has no place to question or do anything beyond what they are told to do. Whereas a helpmate, notices when things need to be done differently or if their partner needs assistance without being asked...they are a partner. Even if Davis may not recognize her strengths, she might consider offering Davis some help when he is struggling or overloaded. If he gets discouraged about something, she can offer encouragement and build him back up. By actively involving herself in his life and constantly being available as a helpmate or gently challenging him to grow, eventually, Davis will grow to respect Elizabeth and recognize her strengths.

QUESTION 2

We are surrounded by media and political movements that raise women up to be strong and independent. This feeds on the woman's misconceived desire to be in control. At our core, women want to be led by a respecting and loving man. Society has painted submission as a wife who stays at home and raises children and obeys her husband's every command (i.e. doormat). But God created marriage to be a partnership, each person having their role in that partnership. The wife is not to be the husband's servant. But ultimately, God has commanded the wife to recognize and respect her husband as the leader of their marriage and family.

QUESTION 3

Personal answers. There are many reasons…wives want to be in control, they don't trust their husbands to make the right decisions, they don't want to suffer the actions of their husband's wrong decisions, their husband refuses to lead, etc. Ultimately, whatever the reason that wives do not submit to their husbands, they have to ask themselves, "do I trust God"? Putting all ifs, ands, and buts aside, if God says in his Word that wives are to submit to their husbands, and if they refuse, do they trust God and do they believe they can take Him at His word?

QUESTION 4

If there is a husband that refuses to lead, remember, a husband cannot take the position of leadership unless that position is vacant. Also remember, wives are to submit JOYFULLY and with a gentle and quiet spirit. This means that they don't tear their husbands down or nag their husbands to lead them. Wives lead by allowing their husbands to lead and encouraging them to lead. If a wife has a husband that is struggling to make a decision, then she should gently guide his decision. For example, if a decision needs to be made about whether or not to purchase a car and the husband can't make a decision, then she should guide him…she can say "I feel like our current vehicles are safe to drive and given our current financial situation, it's probably not the best time to purchase another car. I think we should wait until we absolutely have to buy a new car." More than likely, this will either open up the floor for further discussion or the husband will say "OK, let's do that", then she would follow-up with, "OK, I support your decision." The more times that a husband is given the opportunity to make the decision and verbally hear that his wife supports his decision, the more confident he will grow in making decisions. Wives should continue to let their husbands know that they support their husband's decision…. even if they initially disagreed and shared their reasons and the husband still made a decision they disagreed with. If a wife only submits when they fully agree…then they aren't submitting.

SESSION 5: OUR PERCEPTION OF DECEPTION

FILL-IN-THE-BLANK
1. selfishness, fear, Lying, Withholding, Flattery, Manipulation
2. security
3. crack, yourself, open book, love, grace, selflessness, patience, accountability, wisdom

QUESTION 1

The Results: Many scenarios could arise from this situation. One such scenario is that Nathan feels badly, but in light of the fight that he and Karen got into on the way home, the reasons for his lack of honesty is confirmed. Karen feels betrayed and her security in the marriage and with Nathan is a little shaken. She is drawn one step further from Nathan and one step closer to her best friend…a step that is not good for the marriage. A little resentment on both ends is harbored and without resolution. This pattern of seemingly unimportant dishonest behavior and trust could explode.

Nathan: Aside from his legitimate fears of having to go through another argument with Karen, he should have found a loving way to let her know the dress probably wasn't the best option. If she found out later that he lied to her (which he did) then there was going to be a fight anyway. If she didn't find out that he lied to her, then all he did was facilitate a habit of "white" lies that could cause major issues in their relationship down the road.

Karen: If Karen wants an honest relationship, then she should learn to receive honesty gracefully and not start an argument every time she doesn't hear the answer she was looking for. If she can learn to receive criticism with love, then Nathan would have no reason to fear being honest with her.

QUESTION 2

Sample Answers: You can track any example - hiding money, hiding a whopper mid-day meal, hiding a relationship. Ultimately, when the "truth" does come out, the marriage or spouse is hurt OR because the truth is hidden, the other spouse is not able to assist in that struggle with encouragement OR the deception hinders an individual from being clean and transparent before God (thus hindering his relationship with God) OR the hidden truth sets a foundation and habit in the marriage of deception…which ultimately impacts other areas of the marriage. When these things are considered, the reasons for deception (pride, fear of getting hurt/hurting, fear of accountability – holding on to the flesh, etc) are not worth it.

QUESTION 3

Sample Answer: Let's not look at disagreements negatively. Disagreements are just a way for you to get to know your spouse and understand their point of view better. A marriage that operates as "one" will eventually be so comfortable with each other that they are not afraid to share their feelings, insecurities, worries, fears and struggles with their spouse. They are able to share all of who they are with their spouse and have someone they can fully confide in and do life with.

QUESTION 4

Sample Answer: It's important to use wisdom in regards to "open and totally honest" in your marriage. Being totally honest does not mean degrading your spouse, insulting them or letting them know everything that they do wrong. It's OK to talk about important issues in their behavior, but honesty does not mean nagging. If you have been honest, then commit to praying for your spouse. Every person has many positive and negative qualities, being honest does not mean focusing only on the negative qualities in your spouse.

In regards to accountability: being completely open and honest does not necessarily mean confessing to your spouse every time you pass by a person of the opposite sex that you find attractive – this can be just as damaging to your marriage. However, if you find that "finding someone to be attractive" has turned into a pattern of lust in your life, this may be an area that you need to confess to your spouse for accountability. However, if you don't feel your marriage has an "atmosphere of accountability" yet, then confide in a pastor or spiritual mentor at your church (of the same gender) for further counsel. By no means do we condone keeping any secrets of any kind from your spouse; but great wisdom needs to be taken when dealing with deceptions that are already embedded within your marriage. Every situation is different in how it should be handled and we encourage anyone needing advice on their specific situation to seek spiritual counsel.

SESSION 6: FIGHTING FAIRLY

FILL-IN-THE-BLANK
1. different, decide, reasons, battle, angry
2. willing
3. Responding, speaking, Empathize, Support, Encourage, Fix
4. Topic, resolve
5. Well-being, respect, submit, good, Counseling, discuss, force, Grace, Time, pray, love, Forgive, assist

QUESTION 1
The Results: Nothing was resolved and when Bella addressed "the issue", instead of sticking to what was really bothering her, she made her rounds to everything she could think of that ever annoyed or upset her – this wasn't communicating concisely. Obviously, Jake was refusing to "consent to communicate" and Bella wasn't "communicating calmly" with her emotional outbursts. Although Bella shelved the issue - she just stopped talking about it - but seeds of bitterness could have been planted and the issues may resurface continually until Bella or Jake decide they are tired of dealing with it.

Jake: Because Jake won't talk, it's difficult to say what is causing his silence – whether he doesn't feel he can talk to Bella, or is just lazy, really doesn't have any opinion or is hiding something, is unclear. Regardless, Jake needs to understand that in order for the marriage to grow, he needs to share with Bella whatever is going on inside his head.

Bella: Going off topic, insulting or working herself up into a frenzy doesn't help anyone – if anything, it pushes Jake further into the recesses of his mind. She may want to reevaluate her approach – perhaps she's trying to discuss things at the wrong time? Perhaps she should start with something small – they enjoy hanging out together, so she could try to start on a topic they both agree on and practice "disagreeing" on unimportant issues – like the best football player or what tarter sauce was created to be eaten with. The more Jake becomes comfortable with sharing his opinions on unimportant issues without it turning into a fight, the more comfortable he'll be with sharing more intimate details of his life. Until then, Bella definitely shouldn't force or nag the issue, but continue to love Jake and pray for him.

QUESTION 2
Sample Answer: In secular culture, the best friends are people that make you feel accepted, understood, loved, will never leave you and will never lie to you - where as your spouse does none of those things. We should be our spouse's "best friend" and learn to respond with the goal of understanding our spouse and loving them unconditionally, not just defending ourselves.

QUESTION 3
Personal answers. Cool off for an hour or two, take a nap, reminders to stay on track, etc.

QUESTION 4
Sample Answer: When we disappoint God, He does not accuse, yell, threaten us or leave us. Instead, He is heart-broken for us because He knows that our sin/failure has only taken us further from His love and purpose for our lives. Likewise, we should approach our spouses with the same attitude. When they do something that disappoints us, we should not accuse, yell, blame, freak out, threaten to leave or punish our spouses. Instead, we should first reaffirm that they are loved and accepted by us and no matter how hurt we are, do our best to stand beside and encourage our spouse to overcome their weak areas. Let the failures in your spouse or in your marriage draw the two of you closer together, not further apart. Remember that your spouse does not desire to fail in any area of their life, they want to succeed as your spouse as much as you want them to succeed.

SESSION 7: MORE MONEY, MY MONEY, NO MONEY

FILL-IN-THE-BLANK
1. compare, perspective, God
2. one, together, commitment, role, secrets, together
3. guarantee, growth, blame, hide, encourage, passes

QUESTION 1
The results: Some people may say that it's good that Susan thought ahead and saved up enough money to take care of herself and her kids. Unfortunately, handling their finances differently from the beginning may have resulted in building a stronger marriage instead of ending in a failed marriage, a broken man, a resentful woman and heartbroken children. Sometimes we don't realize how our actions become self-fulfilling prophecies.

Perry: First, it is irrelevant who makes more money. Perry and Susan are "one flesh" and when they married, their family became one unit and their finances should have operated as one unit without anyone keeping track or tallies of who is costing or contributing the most. It's understandable that they wanted things to be "fair", but once the family meshes together, there is no more "fair", all components of the family unit work together in their assigned roles for the betterment of the family. Perry's spending decisions should have been discussed with Susan for the benefit of the entire family, not for just his benefit. He also set a standard that he had the "final say" because he made the most money and not because God gave him the final say. This set up a mode of thinking that if Susan made the most money then she would get the "final say" and gave each spouse the opportunity to spend "their" money without any accountability. This scenario side-steps the issue of Perry and Susan needing to learn how to work together.

Susan: In the beginning, Susan was under the authority of Perry - who made the most money (since Perry had already established that that was the criteria of "head of household"). But once the tables turned, instead of taking the position of head of household, Susan should have had grace on Perry and remained submissive to him. Her continued respect to Perry, even when he contributed nothing financially, would have melted away Perry's previous notions of how the finances and running of the household were ran and he would have submitted himself to taking the position of a "loving leader" instead of a financial tyrant. During a season when Perry's confidence (which was built on his ability to provide for his family) was shattered, Susan should have encouraged him continually. Having Perry remain as the head of household, Susan would not have been burdened with ALL the stress of managing the family. Having a secret account with savings for a "rainy day" already established that if the family went through crisis, instead of working through it together, Susan would be prepared to leave. Saving is encouraged, but saving in secret in the event of a failed marriage is not.

QUESTION 2
Get each couple to answer. It doesn't matter who "handles" finances, but ultimately (after communication and discussion), the husband should make major final decisions about finances with the family's best interest in mind and the wife should respect that decision, even if she doesn't feel it actually IS the best decision for the family.

QUESTION 3
Personal responses. It's important to budget how much your income allows you to spend in each category (clothing, decor, sports, going out, etc). Everyone's answer is different. If you have to accumulate debt in order to get what you want... then it's no good. Encourage each other to be thankful for what you have and wait until you have money in hand to get what you want.

QUESTION 4
Keeping money hidden for the purpose of purchasing a gift or planning a surprise for your spouse is acceptable. Examples of people hiding money: In case their marriage falls apart (as in Susan's case, in which case, they have not fully committed to their marriage), or because they want to purchase or lend money that they know their spouse would not approve of (in which case, they are lying to their spouse and missing an opportunity to learn how to work and discuss things with their spouse.) Prepare yourself for a great marriage, not for an easy divorce.

SESSION 8: PROVING PRIORITIES PRACTICALLY

FILL-IN-THE-BLANK
1. personal, all-consuming, Spouse, God, spouse, People, Task
2. Prioritize, Priorities, Adjustments
3. Sleep, Conversation, Perfection, Changing, Spouse, God's Timing

QUESTION 1
The Results: At this rate, Stephanie may be in danger of losing her family because she has chosen to make her career the highest priority. While this is understandable to an extent during the startup (given the season of opening up a new business), it may not acceptable for a long-term lifestyle.

Ryan: It's great that Ryan is trying to be supportive - especially during the first few months. However, after he realizes that this is becoming a lifestyle, in order for him to demonstrate his priorities (to God, as a leader for his wife and as a father to his children), it may be necessary for him to discuss some major changes with Stephanie and be clear on what is being sacrificed for the sake of her dream long-term.

Stephanie: First, Stephanie should make sure that the bakery was in God's timing and not her own. Secondly, once the startup season has passed, Stephanie should make adjustments to be able to make Ryan and the children a priority - perhaps by hiring additional employees or a manager. One way to make sure she doesn't lose track of her priorities is to never lose sight of her personal relationship with God - even if the season is busy. It's when life gets "too busy" to nurture our relationship with God that we leave ourselves vulnerable to unbalanced priorities. Thirdly, during the times that Ryan and the children attempt to "help out", she should show immense appreciation for her family's support rather than placing "correctly done" tasks into a higher priority in her life.

QUESTION 2
If your spouse loves to go out to eat with you, but instead of taking them out, you are constantly cleaning the house for them....you may feel like you are making them a priority, but in reality, they don't feel prioritized at all. On the other hand, if it's a high priority for your spouse to gain financial freedom and you are coming home every other day with a small gift for them, they will become frustrated that you aren't prioritizing them. Ultimately, if God is our all-consuming first priority, the best way to demonstrate that is to do what He has asked us to do. We can not say that God is our priority and then turn around and treat our spouses harshly or lie about a friend. Take the time to know who is your priority so you can effectively demonstrate their importance in your life.

QUESTION 3
We may know that we have a "calling" to something, but God's timing is not right...so even though our calling is a priority, for that season, it may need to go on the back-burner. If we have a newborn baby, it may be necessary to make that newborn a priority for the first few weeks and our spouses should be understanding of that, but this should only be temporary. Sometimes there are major deadlines in our careers that need to take precedence for a time. We can be making God a priority by spending 4-5 hours in devotion to Him, but be neglecting our other priorities at the same time. Remember, if God is your first priority, then what God desires will also be your priority...and how can we love people and be the spouse or parent He has called us to be if there are no hours in the day left? Most every situation comes with seasons and requires balance and wisdom.

QUESTION 4
Personal answers. If constant communication is important to your spouse, but something you forget easily, then make yourself reminders on your phone to alert you occasionally to say touch base with your spouse.

SESSION 9: EXPECT LESS, APPRECIATE MORE

FILL-IN-THE-BLANK
1. excuses, growth
2. less, you, wrongs, long-suffering, God
3. qualities, complaining, different
4. Tell, others, treat, Assist, feel

QUESTION 1
The Results: Eric refuses to change and Jaclyn expected him to change. The more time that passes, Eric begins to feel more disappointed that the girl who he thought loved him for who he is and hung out with him, is now a nagging wife who is trying to suck all the fun out of his life. On the other hand, Jaclyn doesn't understand when Eric will grow up. At this point, even if Eric changes in response to her incessant nagging, he will probably hold a bitterness about having to give up everything he likes. If he doesn't change, it's not very likely that Jaclyn will continue to "enable" his behavior.

Eric: Eric needs to understand that just because he has "always done something" doesn't mean that it isn't something that he should change. We are in a constant state of change and growth naturally, it's part of maturing. This doesn't mean that he should give up everything he enjoys doing, but he should work with Jaclyn to find a solution that they both agree on.

Jaclyn: Given his behavior while they were dating, Jaclyn should have expected nothing more. She can HOPE that Eric will change and mature and have discussions about it with him, but to determine in her heart that she will not accept him or love him if he does not fulfill her expectations is detrimental to her marriage. Aside from the occasional reminder or conversation regarding a need for change in his behavior, she should focus on his good qualities. She agreed to marry him for a reason, so there are at least a handful of things that she likes about Eric. If she chooses to focus on those things and let God deal with things that need to be changed, her life will be much less stressful and her opinions of her new husband will be much more positive.

QUESTION 2
Once we admit a fault in ourselves without placing blame, then we are faced with the challenge of changing our behavior. If we simply place blame or make excuses, we never have to worry about changing.

QUESTION 3
If you decide to not do your part of the relationship because your spouse isn't doing their part, this will only create greater division, bitterness and a greater stubbornness to not change in both spouses. If you decide to nag or "force" your spouse into changing, this will cause your spouse to also grow bitter and resentful over time even if the results seem to be in your favor in the immediate future. However, if you continue to serve your spouse in your role with greater fervency, God says, eventually, your spouse will be won over by your love with a willing heart for both parties and without bitterness. This doesn't mean that you can't discuss with your spouse areas that could use improvement, but these conversations should be informative and not to be used to force your way.

QUESTION 4
Depending on our spouses to make us happy, to encourage us EVERY TIME, to never disappoint us (Point: our spouses cannot be God for us... Build a personal relationship with God and you'll be able to extend more grace to your spouse for what they are not able to fulfill in you because you are fulfilled in Christ.)

SESSION 10: INTIMATE APPAREL

FILL-IN-THE-BLANK
1. sex, health, desired, confidence, exclusively, together, unbiblical
2. give, take, friendship, sacrifice, focused, mentally, emotionally, physically
3. gift, desired, limitations, ransom, pleasure
4. spouse, special
5. mood, purpose
6. option, options
7. asked, obedience

QUESTION 1

The Results: Because Amy is using sex as a tool to control Clay and Clay allows it, Clay is not allowed to step into a position of leadership in his family and Amy is not experiencing the fullness of a husband who loves her...and not just for sex. Eventually, Clay will turn to other means to satisfy him sexually or he'll become sexually frustrated which will resonate in other areas of his life. Amy will create a self-fulfilling prophecy for herself. She looks down on Clay because of his "obsession" with sex, she then uses sex as a tool to manipulate Clay and it will further cause her to respect him less until she grows annoyed and pities him....all while she continues to feel increasingly more "unloved" by Clay.

Clay: Clay should not allow himself to be controlled by sex...as ultimately, this will cause him to lose any respect Amy may have for him as the leader of his family and marriage. As hard as it may be, Clay should continue to love Amy, but not allow her to manipulate him into making decisions that may end up hurting the family. Clay also needs to understand that simply desiring to have sex with Amy, does not make her feel special. In order for Amy to feel special and have a desired "romantic" component to their marriage, Clay should find different ways to communicate to Amy how amazing and unique she is in his life.

Amy: First, Amy should understand that sex is very important in a marriage and Clay's "obsession" with sex is not so much a perversion as it is a necessity of life for him. If sex is important to him and he is to be a priority in her life as her husband, then she should make sex a priority in her life. Secondly, sex should never be used as a playing piece. The Bible states that her body is not her own but it belongs to her husband and that there should be no withholding of sex for reasons beyond prayer and fasting, if both parties agree upon those terms. She not only causes herself to lose respect for her husband, but she also strips him of his ability to lead his family effectively and because he doesn't feel desired by her, his confidence in their marriage and in life also diminishes. She should consider if getting what she wants in that moment is worth belittling her husband down to the level of a dog. Romantically, although Amy would probably prefer that Clay be "romantic" on his own - without instruction, Amy should try to understand that this may not come naturally for Clay and she may need to tell Clay the different ways that he can make her feel special - especially since how someone feels special and loved differs from person to person.

QUESTION 2

Personal answers. Some examples follow based on the presupposition that wives are not as sexually charged as their husbands and husbands do not tend to be as romantic as their wives (which isn't always the case): Wives can communicate how her husband can relieve her stress so she isn't so exhausted by the end of the night; husbands can give wives a "heads up" so that wives can be mentally prepared; husbands can assist his wife with night chores prior to bed so she doesn't feel exhausted by the time she hits the bed; wives can be proactive and leave themselves reminder notes throughout the day to think of their husbands sexually so that by the end of the night, she is "in the mood"; a husband can make reminders for himself to do something "sweet" for his wife ("I love you" on her FB wall, a text message, stopping by the office, doing the dishes, etc); every time a husband thinks about sex, he can train himself to remember that his wife wants romance as much as he wants sex, prompting him to let her know that he is thinking of her.

QUESTION 3

Think of your attraction for someone as a single tangible object, once that attraction is given to something or someone else physically, mentally or emotionally (porn, romance novels, "emotional" affairs), then you can no longer give that attraction to your spouse. When that happens, the guilty party will begin to try to change their spouse to make them attractive, when in reality, their spouse doesn't need to change, they have simply given their "attraction" to something else so it is no longer available for their spouse.

Many couples claim that watching porn together as a couple makes it easier to "get in the mood." While this may be true, it is also true that the illegal drug Ecstasy will do the same thing. Interviews from Ecstasy-users reveal that the major problem they face is that sex without Ecstasy becomes dull and lifeless because they have experienced sex with Ecstasy. Similarly, while watching porn with your spouse may make sex "better" it will also make sex without porn seem less exhilarating and it will become necessary to have porn be an active part of your sex life with your spouse... not to mention the open door to begin relying on porn privately without your spouse. Much like the serpent told Eve in the Garden of Eden when he was tempting her to eat the apple: yes, by eating the apple she would know what God knows and she would be exposed to a greater range of experiences beyond what her innocence allowed her to prior to "the fall." However, with that knowledge and experience also came sin, death, pain, disappointment, shame, etc. As with all of Satan's tactics, porn may be more satisfying temporarily, but ultimately it leads to destruction and will require a long process of healing once you realize that you have gone too far. Not to mention, inviting porn into your home, even if viewed together, as a couple, would almost certainly be considered sin and the viewer(s) would be indulging in and glorifying that blatant sin.

QUESTION 4
Personal answers, explore the different love languages from Gary Chapman's "The Five Love Languages", finding out from someone else that your spouse has been bragging on you, flowers, an unexpected visit from your spouse, a public declaration on social media, discuss practical examples (cooking a surprise breakfast).

SESSION 11: WHAT'S LOVE GOT TO DO WITH IT?

FILL-IN-THE-BLANK
1. spirit, soul, body, Biologically, Mentally, Spiritually
2. physically, emotionally, emotion, right
3. self-sacrificing, emotion
4. Protecting, Target
5. accept, avoid, Focus, guard

QUESTION 1
The Results: Unless they come to the realization that the temporary fulfillment of their emotions are not worth the destruction that is involved, this cycle will more than repeat itself both with Jason and Erica with Nick. Unfortunately, they live in a false reality, believing that if they are able to have more of what they want, they'll be happy. But in the end, their pursuit of themselves will leave them empty and hurt.

Jason: Although Jason may not realize it, his relationship with porn is probably the cause of his critiques of Erica and his decreased longing for her. Instead of focusing his emotions and desires on Erica, by focusing on his addiction, he has taken those emotions from Erica. Because he fills so much of his time lusting after the women and activities in porn, without realizing it, he has convinced himself that in order for him to have the same excitement for Erica, Erica needs to be and act comparable to what he sees in porn. This mindset leads him to be critical of her in other areas of who she is and of course, although she may try for awhile, no matter what Erica does, she will always fall short of Jason's expectations because she can not reinvent herself into something and someone new like porn can. If Jason is not able to stop looking at or fantasizing about porn, he should seek professional help. (Following the steps to "Recover Your Emotions")

Erica: Yes, it would appear that it is Jason's actions that drive Erica away. However, how Erica responds to her marital problems is no less wrong than Jason's addiction to porn. Lust may manifest itself in different ways, but it is still the same lust. First, Erica should have guarded herself from entering into potentially adulterous relationships by not confiding or developing a personal friendship with someone of the opposite sex in the first place. There is a huge difference, but a fine line between being friendly and being friends. Secondly, just because Erica and Nick had not entered into a physical affair, does not mean that she was not in an adulterous relationship. We can classify Erica and Nick's relationship as an "emotional affair". In God's eyes, emotional affairs are the equivalent to physical affairs (Matthew 5:27-28). As in the situation with Jason, Erica has also shifted her emotions from Jason to Nick, which leads to her being critical of Jason and using his faults as justification. What she believes to be "true love" is just a form of lust, that is temporary and eventually, no matter how perfect of a husband Nick may be, Erica will remain the same and will be prone to developing the same type of emotional affair with someone else. Ultimately, Erica's actions have nothing to do with her situation or her husband, it has everything to do with her and her weaknesses - her lack of self-control. Erica needs to admit her weaknesses and protect herself from being in a relationship where these emotions can develop again. As far as her relationship with Jason, although it may seem hard, Erica should have adopted a mentality of long-suffering and supported Jason and encouraged him to get help as a loving wife.

QUESTION 2
In TV dramas and romantic movies, the notion of someone defying all odds and logic to chase after the person they "truly love" is vastly popular. In fact, it's an extreme rarity to find a scenario in media that depicts someone showcasing true self-sacrificing love and denying their overwhelming desires and emotions. The "happily ever after" that cultural media portrays is one that screams "you'll never be truly happy unless you do what you are feeling!" This concept has trickled down and impacted our individual marriages. So when we, in our marriage, develop a desire for something or someone else, contrary to what we know God's Word tells us, we convince ourselves that the object of our affection is what we "truly love" or we begin to unfairly compare our spouses to whatever it is that is holding our affection at that time - truly believing that if our spouses measure up or if we are able to be with our "true love" that we will find happiness for the rest of our lives....as all media portrays. Unfortunately, this is only an illusion that is only revealed once we have already destroyed our lives in pursuit of our emotions and left a path of tears and destruction in our wake - usually without a chance of restoration except for God's grace.

QUESTION 3
Personal answers. Anything that promotes behaviors opposite of the list in I Corinthians 13 can be used as an example. The idea is to establish that we cannot make decisions based on our feelings because those things are part of our flesh and can be very convincing and easily deceived.

QUESTION 4
Some people find that same (temporary) passion with someone else, they may start blaming their spouse for their imperfections and remain in this state of resentment or they may just ignore it and remain content to live in a "roommate" marriage as long as their spouse expresses no objections. However, instead of finding a replacement, placing blame or avoiding the problem, the first thing a person should do is focus on God and ask Him to reveal an area in their own life to see if they have placed their emotions in someone or something else that has diluted their emotions towards their spouse. Secondly, they should begin focusing on the fruits of love as listed in I Corinthians 13 and avoid the people or things that take their focus away from God and their spouse. As they practice obedience, despite how they feel, their emotions will begin to align with God's Word naturally and they will begin to feel like they love their spouse again.

SESSION 12: ONE
PAGES 67-72

FILL-IN-THE-BLANK
1. singular, living organism, singular living organism, separate, include, one, differences, Dream, Synchronize, Touch, out there, unity
2. together, divorce
3. Passes, Obedient, forgiveness, grace, reconciliation, Wasted
4. closer, individual, destiny

QUESTION 1
The Results: Although divorce has never been an option for Sean and Abby, their marriage is not indicative of what God intended for them. Simply staying together is not enough to have a successful marriage. Sadly, although they legally have a spouse, both Sean and Abby probably feel that something is missing and come short on being able to fulfill the full purpose God may have on their lives. That's not to say that they can not or are not being used by God in their current situation, but they could be missing out on important elements to their destiny and to the happiness that God intended them to have through the complete unity of their marriage.

Sean: Sean must be going through some emotions regarding his father's medical condition...which he should share with Abby so she is in a position where she can support him emotionally. As for the work promotion and the ski-boat, these are both topics that should be thoroughly discussed with Abby before a decision can be made. One of the major benefits of having a spouse is to get a different perspective so we can make the most balanced decisions in our life.

Abby: The same goes with Abby. Her decisions and dreams should be shared and discussed with Sean.

Although not mentioned in the story, assuming their sex life is reflective of their lifestyle, Sean and Abby have removed the safeguards that marriage provides for sexual purity by not engaging in sex with each other regularly. It's not just about Sean and Abby's ability to discuss decisions together and confide in each other emotionally, but also about them sharing and doing life together. Since they do not go out together at all, they are missing one of the greatest blessings of marriage...lifetime companionship.

QUESTION 2
When our spouses do not have a "say" in what we do with "our" stuff (money, social media accounts, clothing, vision, etc). A spouse cannot say "I can do what I want because it's my _____" because their _____ now belongs to both individuals living and moving as one flesh.

The more that a spouse is prone to think of themselves as an individual entity, making decisions based on how it benefits only them, the more likely they are to continue building a separate life (separate friends, hobbies, money, etc) until eventually the marriage is more of a roommate arrangement than a marriage. It is true, that it may keep the peace temporarily...but it doesn't keep the marriage.

QUESTION 3
Personal answers. Commitment and perseverance through trials instead of checking-out at the first sign of turmoil, total honesty with each other instead of lies and hidden secrets, genuine affection towards one another instead of just begrudged roommates, trust (even rebuilt trust after a time of repentance) when the world says "no second chances", etc.

QUESTION 4
There can be many reasons. Sometimes people get overwhelmed by their circumstances and have a hard time seeing beyond them. Sometimes, they simply get tired of trying and tired of being patient and they don't want to have to wait for God to heal their marriage. Sometimes, they say they are believing God, but there is still something in their personal lives that they are refusing to allow God to transform and because of this, they keep hitting a brick wall. Sometimes, they simply don't trust or don't know what God's Word says about their situation and they attempt to handle things on their own – leading to worse circumstances and bitterness.

Focus on God and pleasing Him (and not so much on begging Him to change your marriage or your spouse). Be willing to fully trust Him and what His Word says and what wise spiritual counsel says rather than what you "feel" or what makes sense to you logically. Don't abandon church or the "place of prayer". Sometimes situations can be so overwhelming in our marriage that we feel completely disconnected and abandoned and have no desire to even think about God, but go to that place of prayer anyway and if nothing else, just show up there and say nothing.

#truth
"Let the wife make the husband glad to come home, and let him make her sorry to see him leave."
@Martin Luther

9 781733 930505